Writing a Modern Jewish History

Writing a Modern Jewish History

Essays in Honor of Salo W. Baron

Edited by
Barbara Kirshenblatt-Gimblett

Essays by
Arthur Hertzberg
Susannah Heschel
Barbara Kirshenblatt-Gimblett
Donald Kuspit
Jonathan D. Sarna
Ariel Segal

Poems by
Robert Pinsky

The Jewish Museum, New York | *Under the auspices of the Jewish Theological Seminary of America*
Yale University Press | *New Haven and London*

Title page: Salo W. Baron, 1947. Portrait Photo Collection, Columbia University Archives and Columbiana Library, Columbia University in the City of New York.

THE JEWISH MUSEUM
Manager of Curatorial Publications: Michael Sittenfeld
Associate Curator: Aviva Weintraub
Publications Assistant: Beth Turk
Manuscript edited by Julie Miller

YALE UNIVERSITY PRESS
Publisher, Art and Architecture: Patricia Fidler
Editor, Art and Architecture: Michelle Komie
Manuscript Editor: Susan Laity
Art Book Production Manager: Mary Mayer
Photo Editor and Assistant Production Coordinator: John Long

The Jewish Museum
1109 Fifth Avenue
New York, New York 10128
thejewishmuseum.org

Yale University Press
P.O. Box 209040
New Haven, Connecticut 06520–9040
yalebooks.com

Text designed by Barbara Williams
Set in Janson and Bodoni types by BW&A Books, Inc.

Jacket designed by Richard Hendel
Printed and bound by Thomson-Shore, Inc.

Library of Congress Cataloging-in-Publication Data
Writing a modern Jewish history : essays in honor of Salo W. Baron/edited by Barbara Kirshenblatt-Gimblett ; essays by Arthur Hertzberg … [et al.] ; poems by Robert Pinsky.
p. cm
Includes bibliographical references and index.
ISBN-13: 978-0-300-10677-0 (alk. paper)
ISBN-10: 0-300-10677-7 (alk. paper)
1. Jews — United States — History. 2. Jews — United States — Identity. 3. Jews — United States — Civilization. I. Baron, Salo Wittmayer, 1895–1989. II. Kirshenblatt-Gimblett, Barbara. III. Hertzberg, Arthur. IV. Pinsky, Robert.
E184.35.W75 2006
973.04′924 — dc22 2006004006

A catalogue record for this book is available from the British Library.

The paper in this book meets the guidelines for permanence and durability of the Committee on Production Guidelines for Book Longevity of the Council on Library Resources.

10 9 8 7 6 5 4 3 2 1

This publication has been made possible by the
Trustees of the Salo W. and Jeannette M. Baron Foundation

Contents

Poems by Robert Pinsky appear throughout the text

ix Foreword
Joan Rosenbaum

1 Introduction
Barbara Kirshenblatt-Gimblett

10 Salo W. Baron and the Writing of Modern Jewish History: Speculations in Honor of His Centennial
Arthur Hertzberg

27 "Facing the New World": What Portraits of Early American Jews Reveal and What They Obscure
Jonathan D. Sarna

36 The Moral Sublime: Jewish Women and Philanthropy in Nineteenth-Century America
Barbara Kirshenblatt-Gimblett

57 Jews of the Amazon: Voices from the Earthly Paradise
Ariel Segal

72 Meyer Schapiro's Jewish Unconscious
Donald Kuspit

91 The Myth of Europe in America's Judaism
Susannah Heschel

107 Notes

117 List of Contributors

119 Index

129 The Jewish Museum Board of Trustees

Samurai Song

When I had no roof I made
Audacity my roof. When I had
No supper my eyes dined.

When I had no eyes I listened.
When I had no ears I thought.
When I had no thought I waited.

When I had no father I made
Care my father. When I had
No mother I embraced order.

When I had no friend I made
Quiet my friend. When I had no
Enemy I opposed my body.

When I had no temple I made
My voice my temple. I have
No priest, my tongue is my choir.

When I have no means fortune
Is my means. When I have
Nothing, death will be my fortune.

Need is my tactic, detachment
Is my strategy. When I had
No lover I courted my sleep.

—*Robert Pinsky*

Foreword

In 1992 The Jewish Museum was the fortunate recipient of a gift from the daughters of the preeminent scholar of Jewish history, Salo W. Baron. Their contribution led to the creation of a series of annual lectures for the general public about American Jewish identity that continues to offer stimulating ideas and adds an important dimension to the museum's programming. The essays and poems gathered here represent seven of the eleven Baron Lectures presented between 1995 and 2004 by scholars from wide-ranging fields. Their diverse and fascinating perspectives on the Jewish experience in the Americas are interpreted in an introduction by one of the contributors, Barbara Kirshenblatt-Gimblett, who provides a commentary on Baron as well as an analysis of the essays. Her piece serves as an excellent conceptual map for the range of inquiry that follows.

With this publication, we are twice blessed, for we have had not only the benefit of the public lectures and the lively exchanges with our audience but also the means of preserving their legacy for years to come. We are honored to have been designated as both the venue for the series and the custodian of this important project.

The individual essays often have a particular relevance to an aspect of The Jewish Museum's collection or one of its temporary exhibitions. Cumulatively, however, this volume offers an especially strong connection to the theme of the museum's permanent exhibition, *Culture and Continuity: A Jewish Journey.* Both the book and the exhibition explore the extraordinary longevity of Jews as a people and the dynamic interaction of continuity and change reflected in strategies for Jewish survival. A visitor to the exhibition can find evidence of this continuity in individual works or in the thematically arranged art and artifacts in the galleries. Readers of this book do not physically experience objects from ancient to modern times, yet they encounter a rich discussion of the breadth of Jewish life that accomplishes a similar goal.

In his stirring essay in this volume the late historian and rabbi Arthur

Hertzberg writes about Salo Baron as his mentor and friend as well as about Baron's influence as a historian and teacher. Baron's ideas are reflected in other essays concerning strategies for the continuous identity of a dispersed people. Jewish "distinction without difference" is a concept noted by Jonathan D. Sarna in his examination of colonial portraits of American Jews. Ideas of "how to maneuver among contradictions" are discussed by Ariel Segal in his essay on Amazonian Jews, and the ability to develop a "uniquely multiform Judaism" is noted by Susannah Heschel in her description of postmodern American culture. These interpretations, along with Donald Kuspit's analysis of Meyer Schapiro's "Jewish unconscious" and Barbara Kirshenblatt-Gimblett's dissection of the convergence of the moral and the aesthetic in the philanthropy of Jewish women in nineteenth-century America, together form a dynamic interplay of ideas that encourages the reader to think deeply about Jewish history and identity. Interspersed among the essays are a superb group of poems by Robert Pinsky that were an integral part of his Baron Lecture in 2003.

I wish to express my gratitude to the trustees of the Salo W. and Jeannette M. Baron Foundation—Tobey B. Gitelle, Shoshana B. Tancer, and Russell S. Knapp—for underwriting our lecture series and this volume so generously. Special thanks as well to Aviva Weintraub, Associate Curator, for her thoughtful production of the Baron Lectures at the museum, and to Michael Sittenfeld, Manager of Curatorial Publications, who has so ably supervised every aspect of the creation of this book. I am grateful as well to Yale University Press for copublishing this volume and for its continuing partnership with the museum. Finally, my deep thanks to the museum's Board of Trustees, whose dedication and encouragement constantly lead us to new challenges and new intellectual horizons.

Joan Rosenbaum
Helen Goldsmith Menschel Director
The Jewish Museum

Writing a Modern Jewish History

ABC

Any body can die, evidently. Few
Go happily, irradiating joy,

Knowledge, love. Many
Need oblivion, painkillers,
Quickest respite.

Sweet time unafflicted,
Various world:

X = your zenith.

—Robert Pinsky

BARBARA KIRSHENBLATT-GIMBLETT

Introduction

What finer tribute to Salo W. Baron could there be than the publication of the lectures delivered in his honor at The Jewish Museum over the past ten years? Ranging over a number of topics, but all concerned in some way with the question of Jewish survival, the essays speak to Baron's magisterial view of Jewish history and his scholarly depth. Born and raised in Tarnów (in the Galician part of the Austro-Hungarian Empire, which is today part of Poland), Baron was schooled in Vienna, where he earned three doctorates (in philosophy, political science, and law) and was ordained as a rabbi. He came to the United States at the invitation of Stephen S. Wise, a leading Reform rabbi and Zionist leader, and joined the Columbia University faculty in 1930. His career spanned the better part of the twentieth century. Interviewed by Joseph Berger for the *New York Times* on his ninetieth birthday in 1985, just four years before his death, Baron stated his intention of completing volumes 19, 20, and 21 of his life's work, *A Social and Religious History of the Jews* (1952–93), adding "with a sly smile, 'I'm an optimist from birth.'"[1]

That optimism informed his work as a historian. For Baron, a Jewish history should not be "lachrymose," a chronicle of persecution and poverty. It should not be anti-anti-Semitic, determined primarily by negative external forces. A Jewish history should be positive, emphasizing moral content: the commitment to collective continuity, creative responses to predicaments, and many and diverse ways of being Jewish—in a word, it should show "the autonomous development of Jewish culture."[2] So durable was Baron's optimism that not even the Holocaust, in which his own parents and a sister perished, could shake it, though he recognized the precariousness of Jewish survival, which he considered the price of being different.

Arthur Hertzberg, who enjoyed a long and warm relationship with Baron and officiated at his funeral, considers what Jewish history meant to Baron in his intimate portrait of the man and the scholar, which constitutes the first essay in this book. Hertzberg is puzzled by two things. First, why did Baron never explain, throughout his vast writings, what he understood to be involved in the writing of modern Jewish history? Second, why did Baron not revise the little he did have to say on the topic in 1937 for the second edition of *A Social and Religious History of the Jews* in 1952? The answer, according to Hertzberg, lies in Baron's conviction that ethics, creativity, and continuity, rather than events, are the heart of Jewish history, no matter how consequential those turning points, catastrophes, dispersals, and revolutions. None of these events should be allowed to determine how modern Jewish history is written or overshadow the ordinary flow of life as a historical subject. For Baron, the great lesson of history is that Jewish survival, from the past to the present, depends on respect for tradition (the continuity of values and practices) *and* a commitment to community—in a word, to continuity despite disruption.

It follows that one of the greatest challenges to Jewish collective survival, for Baron, was Emancipation. While full citizenship and the integration of Jews into the larger society was a major gain, it came at a price: the dissolution of autonomous Jewish community life and the potential for disappearance by assimilation. The Jewish sitters in the portraits discussed by Jonathan Sarna in his essay, originally a lecture given in conjunction with an exhibition of eighty-seven early American Jewish portraits at The Jewish Museum, would seem to offer a test case.[3] Why, asks Sarna, do these portraits give no indication that their sitters are Jewish? Would these sitters have found the absence of Jewish identifiers remarkable? After all, Emancipation and religious liberty meant that Jews were no longer compelled to mark their difference with a special hat or badge or self-imposed costume; they could dress as they pleased and in ways that identified them with others of their class and social standing, Jewish or Gentile. Portraits of Christians during this period were similarly devoid of signs of their religious affiliation. Indeed, artists who painted Christian portraits also painted Jewish ones, and they did so according to the rules of a genre whose iconography marked social rather than religious distinction.

Looking outside the paintings' frames to the synagogue, which controlled every aspect of Jewish religious life at the time, Sarna argues that the portraits do not indicate assimilation or loss. Rather, they function as the synagogues do: although the exteriors of early American synagogues were indistinguishable from those of Protestant churches, their interiors were richly Jewish, from the lavish fittings to the liturgy. Similarly, early American Jews were worldly on the outside and Jewish on the inside.

But were their lives so tightly compartmentalized? After all, it was not uncommon for Christian travelers to visit synagogues and for Christian dignitaries to participate in the dedication of synagogues. Rachel Wischnitzer, in her history of American synagogue architecture, even notes "a seat 'set apart for strangers or Christians.'"[4] And the synagogues were designed by Christian architects. In addition, Jews of standing frequently received Christian guests in their homes, an intermingling that could lead to intermarriage, as in the case of Phila Franks, the daughter of Abigaill Franks, the subject of one of the portraits in the exhibition.

As Max Weinreich so felicitously stated in his history of Ashkenaz, what Jews wanted was not isolation from Christians but insulation from Christianity.[5] Yiddish, like other Jewish languages, arose from a symbiotic relationship between Jews and Christians. In the United States, the Jews in the portraits that are Sarna's subject managed insulation without isolation in a different manner: they held fast to their religious faith and practice, while participating in the larger society in ways that did not necessarily distinguish them as Jews. It is, after all, a hallmark of modernity to think of "religion" as something that can be disentangled from a total way of life.

To say that these Jews were latter-day Marranos would suggest that they were Christians in public and Jews in secret, which they were not. To say that they were assimilated, while not entirely untrue, would also miss the mark. Assimilation, which has been accorded such importance in modern Jewish history, explains too much and too little. To make it the focus of a history of American Jews would be, in Baron's terms, giving it too much weight. There is another way of explaining the phenomenon: what might be called *distinction without difference.* This is precisely why what is "Jewish" about these early portraits cannot be seen in their details. This seeming paradox is what distinguishes the trappings of these early American Jews, both Sephardic and Central European, from the more assertive styles of Jewish visibility we came to expect in the latter half of the twentieth century. Distinction without difference is what marks those as Jews who look no different from Christians of their class, whose tables are as elegant (if invisibly kosher) as those of their Christian neighbors, and whose artistic and musical tastes are similar. The sitters for these portraits were Jews in terms of religious observance in their synagogues and homes. But, it could be said, they were also Jews precisely in regard to practices that were, on their face, no different from those of their Christian neighbors. Consider early-nineteenth-century Jewish cookbooks, which may not announce themselves as Jewish on their title pages but provide instructions for kosher, invisibly Jewish, cuisine.[6] Consider as well the benevolent fairs organized by Jewish women that I discuss in my essay in this volume.

The title of my essay, "The Moral Sublime," refers to the particular way in which the moral and the aesthetic converged in collective philanthropic efforts, most dramatically during the Civil War. Women organized large "sanitary fairs" to raise money to improve the care of wounded soldiers, who were dying unnecessarily because of unhygienic medical treatment on the battlefield. After attending a sanitary fair, a reporter of the period was moved to write: "When duty and pleasure go hand in hand in accomplishing so grand an object as that now before us, there is a moral sublimity in it that challenges the admiration of nations, and does more in establishing the righteousness of a cause than any battle that has been fought and won by our brave soldiers since the opening of the war. All politics, creeds, religions and nationalities are forgotten, and the great people, whether as individuals, they believe in its conduct or not, view in their efforts to give that which ameliorate the horrors and suffering of the occasion, and stamp our city and our country as the most enlightened, liberal, and humane of any of which we have recorded since the creation of the world."[7] Not only were Jews active participants in these efforts; they also learned from them how to organize mammoth fairs to support Jewish orphanages, hospitals, schools, synagogues, and other institutions.

If the Jewish fairs were largely indistinguishable from those organized by Christian women, what made them Jewish? How was the strategy of distinction without difference deployed here to specifically Jewish ends? First, philanthropy put a moral and ethical model of Judaism into practice and structured the relationship of well-established American German Jews to their less fortunate, more recently arrived, and more visibly Jewish Eastern European coreligionists. In addition, spectacular fund-raising events required a display of solidarity within an otherwise fractious Jewish community, with its many competing groups and institutions. These events were also prime occasions for demonstrating Jewish self-sufficiency and public-spiritedness. And finally, these fairs offered a model for an inclusive public sphere, with a place for men and women, young and old, rich and poor, Jews and Christians. The fairs were widely covered in both the Jewish and the general press; there was nothing hidden about the Jewish nature of these events, which were organized by Jews on behalf of Jewish causes. As the nineteenth century wore on, holidays that German Jews once celebrated primarily in the home came increasingly to be the focus of large public events held in the biggest spaces in the city: academies of music, opera houses, and armories. Hanukkah pageants and Jewish benevolent fairs were timed to coincide with the Hanukkah and the Christmas shopping seasons, while Purim balls combined holiday celebration with social and charitable goals. The organization of religious observance and social life around philanthropy was guided by the desire to create and demonstrate Jewish solidarity on the one hand and social integration on the other. These desires were not necessarily in conflict or compartmentalized. On the contrary, the fairs attempted to harmonize them and to do so in public, in ways consistent with the sensibility of their participants.

No one could be further from the New York Jews who ran the benevolent fairs than the "Jewish mestizos" who are the subject of Ariel Segal's essay. While most of the essays in this volume are concerned with mainstream American Jewry and normative Judaism, Segal's concentrates on Iquitos, an isolated city in the Peruvian rain forest, where he finds a surprising answer to the eternal question of what it is to be a Jew. During the 1880s rubber boom, Jews from North Africa, most of them men, came to this city, accessible then only by riverboat. In time, they intermarried with indigenous women. When the rubber industry collapsed just before World War I, many of the men left, in some cases leaving their families behind. The Jewish Society of Iquitos, which was formed in 1909, declined, although a Jewish cemetery survived. There was no synagogue or rabbi, contact with the Jews of Lima was intermittent, and the community became increasingly isolated.

By all rights, these Jews should have been absorbed into the indigenous society. But instead they created a syncretic culture combining Jewish, indigenous, and Catholic elements. They observed the Jewish Sabbath, but many also attended church; tombstones in the Jewish cemetery may bear both a Star of David and a cross. In these and other ways, the "Jewish mestizos" of Iquitos remembered their Jewish ancestors. Above all, they felt Jewish. Thanks to improved communication after World War II, these Amazonian Jews began to enter the Jewish mainstream. They revived the Israelite Society of Iquitos and became interested in formal conversion to Judaism and immigration to Israel. By the time Segal, a Venezuelan Jew, arrived in 1995, there were about 150 Jewish descendants in Iquitos, a city of 400,000.They had become, in Segal's terms, "obsessed" with being Jewish, and he became obsessed with them.

"They know how to maneuver among contradictions," Segal writes. But as he is quick to note, what appears inconsistent and contradictory to him may not appear so to them. Thanks to the sensibility that Segal brought to these Amazonian Jews, they appeared to him as postmodern *avant la lettre.* But their attraction to him was of a different order. He was their ticket to normative Judaism; they wanted him to teach them Hebrew and Jewish liturgy.

No other essay in this volume approaches the question of what it means to be a Jew from a case as extreme as that of the Iquitos mestizos. The Jewish mestizos prompt Segal to formulate an expanded notion of Marranism (considered by some the model of Jewish survival), one that is not confined to a particular historical episode but refers to a wider phenomenon and to periods and places other than the Iberian Middle Ages. Segal proposes that Marranism arises not only from forced conversion (and the secret practice of Judaism) but also from "the natural assimilation of a religious system that coexists with a group's original Jewish heritage without eclipsing it." What Segal finds so attractive in Marranism, as he conceives it, is the idea of a dual identity, with Judaism the dominant point of reference, persisting under the most improbable of conditions.

Far from the Amazonian rain forest, Meyer Schapiro, the subject of Donald Kuspit's essay, also found the idea of "maneuvering among contradictions" useful as a way of understanding both the Jew and the creative artist. A distinguished art historian who wrote about Romanesque as well as modern art, Schapiro was born in 1904 in Šiauliai (in modern-day Lithuania) and immigrated to the United States as a child. He received his doctorate in art history from Columbia University and joined the Columbia faculty in 1928. While Schapiro was unequivocally Jewish, he rarely mentioned Jews or Judaism in his work. Exceptions include a laudatory essay on Marc Chagall's Bible paintings and a critical assessment of Bernard Berenson, the connoisseur of Italian Renaissance art, who converted from Judaism to Christianity and had nothing good to say about Jews and their artistic capacities. Berenson became Schapiro's Other. A man of questionable provenance himself, Berenson became the authenticator of artists whose provenance was questionable.

Given the absence of Jewish references in his writing, what makes Schapiro's work Jewish? To answer this Kuspit plumbs the "Jewish unconscious" in Schapiro's work, which he locates in a particular disposition arising from the alienation built into Jewish existence. It is not Jewish solidarity—and certainly not subservience to orthodoxies of any kind, including Jewish ones—that captures Schapiro's imagination but the dissidence of a Jewish minority in a Christian world. This disposition is marked by "creative survival against great odds," heterodoxy, and an ability to hold contradictions in suspension. Characterizing this condition as alienation reveals the failure of modernity to alter the fundamentals of the Jewish condition while valorizing the Jewish predicament and identifying it with the situation of the artist and modernity itself.[8]

Not only have Jews played a signal role in making art modern; their artistic engagements have been important in making Jews modern.[9] In Kuspit's reading of Schapiro, to be modern is "to be alienated from one's received identity." Qualities that might otherwise be considered deficiencies become assets from the perspective of modern art. They come to define not only the creative artist but also the kind of art history that Schapiro himself practiced and the place of

Jews within it. Schapiro was not alone in this approach. In a lecture delivered at The Jewish Museum and published in *Commentary* in 1966, the art critic Harold Rosenberg argued that Jews have played a central role in creating "a genuine American art" precisely because they created it as individuals, not as representatives of a particular group. The result is "Jewish creation in art," which, while "not a Jewish art, is a profound Jewish expression." What matters to Rosenberg is that "while Jewish artists have not been creating as Jews, they have not been working as non-Jews either. Their art has been the close expression of themselves as they are, including the fact that they are Jews, each in his individual degree."[10]

Such understandings are part of a long history of creatively imagining what it means to be a Jew. That history includes the changing relationship of American Jews to their European past, the subject of Susannah Heschel's essay in this volume. Was America the Promised Land, whose "democratic principles embodied the true moral essence of Judaism," or an assimilationist threat? Was Europe a place of persecution, stifling Orthodoxy, and subservience to Christianity, or a source of authentic Judaism? How was one imagined in terms of the other?

Heschel, like others in this volume, challenges assumptions about assimilation as a road leading inevitably to disappearance. Following Baron, she takes inspiration from the Marranos. Once in New Amsterdam, the Dutch Marranos who fled Brazil in 1654 persisted in their private Jewish observance, not because they were forced to but because private observance had become their tradition. Their conversion to Christianity had prepared the way for them to hold high office in European civil society, the military, and the church, all of which, according to Heschel, "accustomed them to positions of honor and authority, not subservience." Following from this, they were prepared to stand up for their rights. Coming early in the history of Jewish life in America, these New World Marranos, Heschel writes, "set a pattern of political and cultural self-assertion" that subsequent generations of Jews, no matter where they came from, would follow, a pattern that was stronger in the United States than in Europe.

For Heschel, nineteenth-century Protestant America held out hope for the creation of a liberal Judaism that was informed by democratic principles and less vulnerable to anti-Semitism. One reason was the relative lack of interest in formal theology among Christians and therefore less inclination to articulate theological anti-Judaism. While there were other reasons for the Protestants' religious tolerance, Heschel stresses the important role that Judaism played in prompting considerations of religious pluralism. How Jews responded to these circumstances, whether Reform rabbis in the nineteenth century or, in the twentieth century, Reconstructionists, American Zionists, secular Jews, and Jewish intellectuals, reveals a richness of possibilities for imagining American Judaism that cannot be reduced to the simple binary vision of America as either Promised Land or land of assimilation.

Above all, for Heschel, it is the legacy of assertiveness, established by the New Amsterdam Marranos, that holds the key to such momentous developments in Jewish life as the ordination of women, the involvement with social and political movements, and especially what she calls "a uniquely multiform Judaism" within a multicultural and postmodern America. This development warrants attention from Europe and Israel, given the increasingly important role of the Muslim and Arab world, in addition to the Christian one, in how Jews see themselves and those around them. This essay, like the volume as a whole, affirms not only Baron's vision of the great variety of Jewish experience but also his conviction that Jewish pluralism – the many ways of being Jewish – may well be the key to Jewish survival.

Antique

I drowned in the fire of having you, I burned
In the river of not having you, we lived
Together for hours in a house of a thousand rooms
And we were parted for a thousand years.
Ten minutes ago we raised our children who cover
The earth and have forgotten that we existed.
It was not maya, it was not a ladder to perfection,
It was this cold sunlight falling on this warm earth.

When I turned you went to Hell. When your ship
Fled the battle I followed you and lost the world
Without regret but with stormy recriminations.
Someday far down that corridor of horror the future
Someone who buys this picture of you for the frame
At a stall in a dwindled city will study your face
And decide to harbor it for a little while longer
From the waters of anonymity, the acids of breath.

—Robert Pinsky

ARTHUR HERTZBERG

Salo W. Baron and the Writing of Modern Jewish History

Speculations in Honor of His Centennial

Salo W. Baron at the lectern, c. 1940s. Photograph by Virginia Stern. From the Ratner Center for the Study of Conservative Judaism, Jewish Theological Seminary, XE2271/P3232.

My life has been interwoven with the life of the Baron family since the winter of 1940–41. That year I arrived in New York as a student at the Jewish Theological Seminary and quickly wangled permission to take courses at Columbia under Dr. Baron. Baron's wife, Jeannette, immediately befriended me, and soon the door of their house was open to me. I became part of the family as the Baron children were growing up. Our four-year-old daughter was the flower girl at Tobey Baron's wedding, which took place in 1957 at Temple Emmanuel, our synagogue in New Jersey. It was the first wedding in Temple Emmanuel's not-quite-completed building.

I remember with emotion that when Jeannette died, my wife, Phyllis, and I were in Paris, and we had difficulty getting back. I suggested on the telephone that the family not wait for us, but they insisted that I had to officiate at the funeral. The funeral was held a day later. When Salo died, there was no question that it would be my duty and honor to read the service and say whatever I could on that occasion. So on this occasion, the celebration of his centennial, I, as his student, as someone who received his doctorate under him, as someone who succeeded him as president of the Conference on Jewish Social Studies and worked with him and under his direction in innumerable tasks both scholarly and communal, and also as someone whom he and his wife took into their family, consider it a particular honor, and a particular necessity, to give this talk.[1]

One of the things that most impressed me about Baron was that he was capable of expressing some very sharp opinions about people, especially after I came to know him better. He liked some people and didn't like others, thought well of some and little of others, despite their public reputations. But what I found astonishing about him was that occasionally, when the subject would turn to scholarly work, he might speak objectively and with great respect about the work of people whom he had just derided personally. He might also be critical of people of whom he had just spoken with affection. I once asked him, "How can you do this?" and he replied, "I make a very clear distinction between personal relations and objective truth, as near as I can figure it."

Often when I talked to Baron, I thought of my father. They were both Galician Jews, born in the same year. Their cultural formation was similar, but my father became the Orthodox Hasidic Rav in Baltimore and Baron a famous historian and seemingly—and I will explain why I say *seemingly* in the course of this essay—secular person. I once asked my father the same question: "Why do you speak so well of so-and-so's [Torah] scholarship when you can't stand him?" And he said, "There is a passage in the Talmud that says that whatever you may feel about someone else, once you enter the house of study the only criterion is truth." It is in that spirit that I want to write about Baron. That I loved and admired him, I think should be abundantly clear. But I was also critical of him. And I shall say some things that are not completely complimentary. He was too great a man, too great a historian, to demand uncritical admiration.

Let me start with the fact that he gave everyone who knew him an inferiority complex. I remember coming in one day to talk about the dissertation I was planning to write on the history of the Jews in France in the eighteenth century. Baron asked me the inevitable question a professor asks a doctoral student: "What are your sources?" I proceeded to describe those I knew about, to explain where I hoped to look for others, and so on. When we made the appointment he had known only that I was going to be researching Franco-Jewish history in the eighteenth century, but he proceeded to make a monkey of me. Off the top of his head he could refer to many more sources, and discuss them in depth, than I had found after a year or more of digging.

When I told my friend Menahem Schmelzer that story, he mentioned that he had spent ten years working under Baron's direction, putting together a catalogue of extant medieval Hebrew manuscripts in the various libraries of the world. He was creating it from a bunch of little chits of paper that the bibliographer, Aaron Freiman, had left behind. When Schmelzer was hired he had thought that Baron would benevolently look over his work occasionally, but figured that he could not have any deep knowledge of this highly technical field.

He discovered that week after week, for ten years, Baron would be able to ask him questions or give him further information about every one of those *tzetelach* (chits of paper). If you thought you knew something, all you had to do was talk to Baron to find out that you needed to go home and study some more. Then, perhaps, you could arrive at a respectable level of ignorance.

I know what Baron considered the ideal life. Digging about in his writings to prepare this essay, I read thousands of pages, and I found the key to his philosophy in an essay he published in an unusual place: *Great Ages and Ideas of the Jewish People*, edited by Leo Schwartz.[2] Baron's essay in that book is one of two places in which he put together an account of modern Jewish history. In the essay he quotes Maimonides on how to live a good life – not a good life for a scholar of the Torah, but a good life for anybody: spend a maximum of three hours a day earning a living, and study Torah for a minimum of nine hours a day. Anyone who knew Baron or knows something about him, will recognize that he was speaking autobiographically – though I suspect that he thought that the nine hours were for laypeople; his graduate students should add three more. He, of course, believed that he ought to study for fifteen hours a day. And he did, until a few months before the end of his life.

What did Baron teach? What are the clues to his understanding of modern Jewish history? I would like to suggest four. The first is an interesting proposition offered in the first edition of his *Social and Religious History of the Jews* and repeated in the second edition.[3] If you compare the texts, you will find only one chapter that is unchanged from one edition to the next. In the first edition, which he wrote in the mid-1930s, based on a series of lectures he had given at Columbia on the interplay between social conditions and religion, he wrote that he did not believe that the Nazis would become worse than they already were. He did foresee the war, but he believed that if Germany went to war and conquered Ukraine (another of his prescient guesses), it would thereby become a multiethnic empire, and the Nazis would have to tone down their racism and conditions might even improve. Between the first edition and the second, World War II intervened, along with the Shoah, the destruction of European Jewry. His parents, who were alive when the war broke out and whom he desperately tried to save, were now gone. And whatever was left of the Wittmayer and Baron patrimonies in Galicia, in southern Poland, had disappeared. And yet he reprinted that first theoretical chapter verbatim.

I think that chapter is one of the keys to what Baron felt about modern Jewish history. Once you understand it, the rest becomes clear. What he is saying is that Jewish history – at the beginning, today, and in the future – is the triumph of Jewish experience, the triumph of history over nature. In various permutations, Baron is talking about a people who are going to impose their morality—not an abstract morality revealed once and for all, but an unfolding morality as it is experienced in the flow of life—upon the wickedness of humanity and the unruliness of nature. Jewish history is the progressive unfolding, from age to age, under changing circumstances, of a communal morality reaching out toward an example of moral behavior, moral possibility, for all of the world.

Let me quote one of the key sentences. I repeat, this comes in both editions: "Justice, and especially social justice, remained throughout the ages the cornerstone of Jewish public life and theology."[4] And so for Baron, whether before or after the Holocaust, Jewish history is not about tragedy. He denied over and over again the thesis that Jewish history was *Literatur und Leidensgeschichte*, "literature and suffering." He denied the notion of "and so they beat on us, and so they beat on us." He insisted, on the contrary, that expulsions and pogroms were simply miserable interludes that highlighted the important theme of Jewish history: the capacity of Jewish life to regenerate itself. For Baron, before and after the Holocaust, the meaning of Jewish history remains the same: the taming of the wildness in human beings within nature in the name of moral conduct; not morality in the abstract, but public morality.

Baron believed that the Jews were a people who, by their conduct, make a moral difference. This idea took him back to the oldest biblical images. I would like to add one that I suspect he would use today, if we were privileged to have him writing his own version of his historical vision. My image is not of Joseph living in Egypt, which Baron cites—Joseph *in* the culture yet not quite *of* it; nor is it the image of Amos, rebelling against the worship of power in ancient Israel. I think the image that offers the clearest example of Baron's viewpoint is that of Abraham, who kept all the doors of his tent open to wayfarers. When the angels came to tell Abraham that they were going to destroy Sodom, Abraham did not know who they were. He did not know whether they were friends or enemies. He knew nothing about them. But his tent was open to them. When Abraham learns that God is about to destroy Sodom—a wicked, idolatrous place, very alien to him—he stands before God and says, "Don't do it. It's unjust. Maybe there are a few righteous people left there." In what I've always thought is the greatest verse in the Bible, he says to God, "hashofet kol ha'aretz lo ya'aseh mishpat": "Shall not the Judge of all the world do justice?"

I think Baron saw the Jews as the bearers of a moral vision in difficult times. And this view obligates us to think about the moral vision involved in what we do to those who are alien, who are in deep trouble, who hate one another because they are different. To those people—and to ourselves—I think we need to counterpose the vision of the open tent. I hope that vision can help us trans-

Salo W. Baron with his wife, Jeannette. Special Collections and University Archives Department, Stanford University.

form our own hatreds, our own angers, and our own wars and help us take the lead in teaching and ministering to places and societies that keep people not like themselves outside the door.

I always think of Baron and my father together. My father once said that "and thou shalt love thy neighbor as thyself" could not have been written about a neighbor who was a nice, decent, reasonable person like oneself, because then it stood to reason. We are commanded to love our neighbor as ourselves even when our neighbor is a rotten, impossible, alien, difficult, and belligerent person. At that point, God tells us that we ought to represent the law of openness, the law of concern.

Now this vision of Jewish history is not the same as the Reform idea of "the mission of Israel," because Baron is not describing an abstract religious community. He is explaining a living people whose vision persists throughout Jewish history. He is asserting a vision that makes the Jewish people the moral elite (he is not ashamed to use the word) of mankind. And he is not even afraid of making a nod toward Freud in the opening chapter to his history, asserting boldly that Jewish morality is expressed in the Freudian notion that the id must be conquered by the superego. That is, the Jews are the representative people. Whether it is Moses coming down from Sinai bringing moral teachings instead of words about power, or Amos announcing (I am quoting Baron as he quotes), "Only you have I known from all the nations of the earth, therefore, you must be particularly an example of the most delicate and sensitive morality—a morality which is universal," Baron insists on this moral and elite responsibility as the center of Jewish history.

Now this will surprise some who have read Baron's works only superficially. I don't know anyone who has lately read all eighteen volumes of *A Social and Religious History of the Jews*. One reads him for hardheaded things, for descriptions of the interplay of social and religious factors in Jewish history. But one has to begin with the historical mystique. If space allowed, I could discuss the roots of Baron's viewpoint in Nachman Krochmal, the earlier Galician theoretician of Jewish history. But I must go on to the next, more difficult, question and the second clue to Baron's understanding of modern Jewish history.

What did Baron make of the Holocaust? How could he say the same thing about the Nazis before and after the Shoah? After all, the Holocaust was not an abstract matter to him. It was a source of the deepest personal pain. Immediately after the war he organized Jewish Cultural Reconstruction, through which he, along with executive secretary Hannah Arendt, tried to save what remained of the Jewish libraries of Europe. Much remained that the Nazis had stolen and despoiled, and Jewish Cultural Reconstruction redistributed hundreds of thousands of books to places where they could be used and where they are still used. Later he accepted the invitation to deliver the historical case for the prosecution during the Eichmann trial. Baron was not insensitive to the Holocaust. He did not pass over its significance. And I will betray a confidence by revealing that there were things that he wanted to rewrite in light of it.

After the Holocaust, Martin Buber had wanted to rewrite a passage in his famous *Drei Reden über das Judentum* (Three addresses on Judaism). In the second speech, using Nietzschean language that was fashionable among the intelligentsia back around 1910, Buber had rooted Jewish experience *in Blut und Rasse*—"in blood and race."[5] Now, those words were still moderately acceptable in 1910, but certainly not in the 1950s. When Buber wanted to have the three lectures translated for publication in English, he asked me to do the translation, and asked me to take out those particular passages. I refused. I said, "What you wrote then deserves a footnote of explanation, but you wrote it. It is part of the historical record, and necessary for the understanding of your own development."

Similarly, Baron once made a tape in which he said that the Nazis could not possibly become any more wicked: that the idea that mass murder was imminent was simply beyond belief. Baron did not know where the tape was, but if he could have found it, he wanted to destroy it. Like all of us—and I am old enough to remember the era—he had wanted desperately to believe that what was happening wasn't happening until we could no longer *not* believe it. But later he knew that it had happened. And he said, in his testimony at the Eichmann trial, that the Shoah was the single greatest tragedy that had ever happened to the Jewish people. And yet his theory of history was not affected.

Why? For two reasons. Baron, for all of his mysticism—and he was more of a historical mystic than most people realize—was essentially a man of the nineteenth century, a rationalist. As a historian, he claimed, "Whatever may be my theological beliefs, whatever may be my mystic views, as a historian I deal in fact." This is how he answered Eichmann's defense attorney Robert Servatius when he was challenged on the witness stand. Baron was a rationalist. When asked to explain anti-Semitism, he answered as Leo Pinsker did after the pogroms of 1881, as Theodor Herzl repeated in his *Der Judenstadt.* Baron said that anti-Semitism is the dislike of the unlike. In other words, the Jews are a visible and enduring minority, and people do not like those who are not like themselves.

Servatius probed further, asking, "Aren't there mystical reasons? Aren't there deep historical reasons that this hatred is so pervasive and so deep?" Servatius was trying to imply that if there were deep tides of anti-Semitism beyond human control, then we should not blame a bureaucratic cog like Eichmann for his actions. And Baron answered, No, it is not beyond human control for the individual to decide what side he is on. I knew about this exchange because it was quoted in the papers, and I remember saying to Baron when he returned home, "You were, of course, quoting Rabbi Akiba's words on the question of free will and determinism, when he said, 'Everything is foreseen, but the individual is responsible.' God foresees everything, and yet the individual is responsible for his choices." Baron, the rationalist, had to believe that rational management could have avoided this horror; if the horror came, it was the responsibility of those who could have done, and should have done, better.

But beyond his rationalism, beyond his desire not to see the demonic, not to see history as something that was basically out of our control, there was a deeper reason, which he never really admitted to. Unlike my other statements about Baron's views, for which I can show written evidence, what I say now has been pieced together from hints found throughout his writings, but if you read enough of his work, you'll find that Baron did not really believe that the Holocaust was unprecedented. It was the greatest tragedy that ever happened to the Jews, but it was not unprecedented. The destruction of the Temple in Jerusalem, not once but twice, was another tragedy. And the first exile, in historical terms, was yet another. For Baron, in the broad sweep of Jewish history, the Holocaust was part of an even greater and deeper phenomenon than the murder of a third of the Jewish people. That broader phenomenon was a profound transformation of Jewish life that is taking place in modern times, a change that was prefigured at these earlier moments in Jewish history, starting with the first exile.

When the First Temple in Jerusalem was destroyed and the Jews went into exile, then the whole of Jewish religion changed. When the Temple was destroyed, there was more than fear, more than sorrow; there was a sense that the enterprise was over, that the priests were no longer in the Temple, that God was no longer in his sanctuary. Jewish life as it had been known, the life of biblical Judaism, was over. At that point, Baron believed, a Jeremiah arose to tell the Jews: build houses, plant vineyards, start your life over again in a new key. In the next five hundred years, through the destruction of the Second Temple, as the Jews became primarily a people in exile, a new Judaism arose in which the Bible was reinterpreted; to a great degree, Baron felt that it was interpreted out of existence. The new Judaism was reacting to a different set of circumstances and conditions: now priests were replaced by rabbis, the Temple was replaced by study, and the Talmud superseded large portions of the Bible or changed them through interpretation. When their historical circumstances have changed radically, the Jews have displayed an enormous and amazing energy to change with them in order to survive. These transformations occurred not only with dislocation, with exile; they also came about with the tragic loss of large parts of the Jewish people – not only to exile but to assimilation, to departure for other reasons, and to destruction.

The Enlightenment and Emancipation changed the conditions of Jewish history as radically as did the destruction of the First Temple. But at the same time Baron believed that the Enlightenment and Emancipation again unlocked enormous energies. For instance, there is a lyrical passage in one of his treatments of modern Jewish history in which he talks of his personal friendships with Hayim Nachman Bialik, the poet; Chaim Weizmann, the first president of Israel; and Albert Einstein. These three men, he claimed, were possible only in an era of Emancipation and Enlightenment. They represented enormous energies and creativity; and they forged a new age in Jewish history. What the definition of that new Jewish age is going to be, I do not know.

In one of his more fascinating insights, Baron used to talk about Karl Marx.

He noted that most people think that Marx departed from the ideology of his grandfather, the chief rabbi of Trier, who was descended from the Katzenellenbogens, one of the great learned Jewish families from Central and Eastern Europe. Baron claimed that this was not the case—in both the moral impulse was the same, flowing from the grandfather, who expressed it through *halacha*, to the grandson, who expressed it through his effort to make class relations in society more just.

So Enlightenment and Emancipation are not, for Baron, simply threats. This isn't Abraham Joshua Heschel's ghetto, in which the Jews *davened* and *shukkeled* until Enlightenment and Emancipation arrived, and bingo! it all disappeared. Baron doesn't believe that the ghetto was ever quite so hermetically sealed to begin with. But, he insists, after it was unsealed, it did not simply disappear. Now, on this point, I tend to be somewhere in the middle. I am more of a pessimist.

Let me relate a personal story, which will illuminate what sort of man he was. Baron knew that my dissertation, which I wrote under his direction, was quite pessimistic about the corrosive aspects of the Enlightenment.[6] (I was then even more of a pessimist than I am now.) Baron disagreed with my views, but unlike many dissertation directors, he allowed me to write exactly what I pleased. He sponsored my dissertation, defended it in the dissertation exam, and nominated it for distinction (which it would have been given had there not been a lesser man in the room who couldn't stand the fact that my views clashed with his). Baron was much more of an optimist than those who look at the Emancipation and Enlightenment and say, "Oy, vey! They're all assimilating out. The door to assimilation has opened, and the only place where Jewish life can survive is in the ghetto." If Jews can live a Jewish life only in the ghetto, then we should close this Jewish Museum, put on *kapotas* (or their female equivalent), and move to Brooklyn. And the more radical among us should proclaim that we are waiting for the Lubavitcher to reappear *bimhayra v'yamaynu*—quickly and in our own day.

Baron did not believe this. There is a wonderful, astonishing passage in which he is bold enough to say that the life of a truly pious Reform Jew—a person who really cares about the doctrine of morality, of concern for the rest of mankind—is as hard to live, or harder, than that of the most rigorously Orthodox Jew. Baron was much more open, much more willing to consider true pluralism, and much more sympathetic and willing to embrace all of Jewish history, than lesser scholars are.

I see in Baron's published vision of Jewish history what his unwritten vision of modern Judaism would have been. I suspect that he was not in a great hurry to write about that vision because he was a man of peace, not a man of war. In that, he was unlike me; I would have written about it. And I no doubt will. But Baron was unwilling to synthesize in one place the things that appear scattered throughout his works, a sentence here, a sentence there. For Baron the Jewish people are undergoing the same kind of transformation in dislocation in the modern age that they did in the past. Between 1890 and 1914, 30 percent moved out of Europe in a vast migration; many assimilated or splintered into parties. This dispersion was followed by the murder of European Jewry in World War II. Yet all these tragedies are part—he almost says, mystically part—of the historical process within which we are again going through the first exile under modern conditions. I can cite Baron's writings on this point. The critical sentence comes in the first edition of *A Social and Religious History of the Jews*, in which he did write about modern Jewish history: "Jewish life is being more transformed, and at a faster pace, than at any time since the first exile."[7] The Shoah, for him, was part of this profound historical transformation.

This brings me to my third clue, which should help us understand what Baron thought this transformation would produce. In the first edition of his history, and again in the second in various places, he says that it is not enough for Jews to fight their enemies. In the first edition he is referring to the Nazis' actions. In the second edition he is referring to the American Jewish preoccupation with anti-Semitism. (I used to think that I was the first to notice this preoccupation, but now I know that I got it from him, during a walk or in a seminar.) There he wrote, "All of the [effort] that we spend on Jewish anti-anti-Semitism is a waste of time. Anti-Semitism is a problem of the majority. The battle can only be fought and won by the majority, and by the nature of the majority society. All of the anti-anti-Semitism endeavors put together aren't worth a nickel." That's Baron on the subject, not Hertzberg; I am merely a pale copy of the master, a somewhat more bellicose version. Baron sets these words in the middle of a long historical paragraph, so that you are not directly confronted by them. But he believed that the transformation of the Jewish people should not make them into an anti-anti-Semitism community. He suggested instead the astonishing proposition that the continuity of Jewish life, even as it sloughs off some forms and adopts others, as it refashions itself, must lie in its positive content, its moral content. For Baron, moral content cannot be safeguarded without halacha: obedience by the community, by individuals as a community, to a set of norms. He even produces the interesting paradox that while we may have trouble with the notion of God in the teeth of modern philosophy and have to refashion our ideas in such a manner that they do not seem to relate to the corpus of the tradition, yet a refashioned Jewish community can practice halacha even with new philosophical ideas about the existence of God. Again, he is talking not about Orthodox halacha, the halacha of Mea Shearim or Brooklyn, but about the notion that Jews must do some tangible things that express their values and their culture and their aspirations together.

Lest you think this is a weird idea that Baron came to late one night because his Orthodox antecedents were bothering him, let me tell you that it is consistent with things said by my great friend Gershom Scholem, the authority on mysticism and Kabbalah. For Scholem, Jewish life is inconceivable without the practice of halacha. The two Jewish luminaries — Baron, the social and religious historian, and Scholem, the intellectual historian, the historian of the Kabbalah — neither of whom could be considered Orthodox in his personal views, nonetheless affirm that the continuity of Jewish life is in some way embedded in the forms of tradition. The idea also has more than a little of Nachman Krochmal and a good bit of Ahad Ha'am in it; it fits the conservative belief that the continuity of Judaism is to be found in those practices and values that bear some relation, even in their transformation, to the past, to what Jews have fashioned throughout our history.

The other defining moment for Jews that occurred during Baron's lifetime — and herein lies the fourth clue to his understanding of modern Jewish history — was the establishment of Israel. Israel was already being formed in the thirties, when he wrote the first version of *A Social and Religious History of the Jews*; and it was a state by 1952, when he was writing the second version. Yet his view of Israel remained the same. He was a Zionist in that he was profoundly committed to the creation of the state of Israel. But — and this is a very important "but" — he was also profoundly moved by the Hebraic culture that was being created there, a culture that he hoped would be rooted in the past. Yet he continued to believe that the Jewish people are essentially rooted in history, not nature. And therefore the worship of even the soil of the renascent homeland, if it became an end in itself, was for him idolatry. He warned that if the land of Israel ever became the end value, then we shall have transformed ourselves into the very idolaters against whom Jewish history was created. We shall have become a worldly people.

In an interesting instance of historical mysticism Baron located the Jewish people post-Holocaust in three centers: the Soviet Union (now the former Soviet Union), America, and at the borders of the Middle East, in Israel. In each of these places, he noted, there is deep instability — in the United States, with its multiethnic tensions; in the Soviet Union, then fighting for the future of communism; and of course in the Middle East, with its chronic unrest. He believed that the Jews involved with these historical problems had been cast in the role of leaders in the creation of a more moral society.

Baron was in no conventional sense a Zionist; although he embraced Zionism, it was not in the sense of Zionist triumphalism. If he were alive and you asked him, "Do you think that the Third Commonwealth will last forever?" he would say, "I hope so, but it's not going to eat up all of Jewish life. And even if it does not last forever, in the nature of Jewish life we will pick ourselves up and refashion something out of our tradition, somewhere else, under changed circumstances." Perhaps we will colonize Mars. There was in him no worship of land qua land. For him land was always the opportunity for Jewish culture and morality.

From age to age the Jewish people re-create themselves in some center of Jewish existence. The last such center was Poland. Baron takes great pains in several places to prove that German Jewry never existed—the German Jews all came from Posen. (He had even less patience with the myth of German Jewry than I do. I was delighted when I discovered this, because I had never understood the paradox that although German Jews spoke Yiddish into the beginning of the nineteenth century and beyond, they were somehow or other *echt deutsch*, "real Germans.") All their rabbis came from Poland. Baron explained that Posen was the great watershed, and he saw Jewish history as moving from center to center, with the last great center in Poland.

The closest I ever found him to tears in his writing was in the essay he wrote for the Schwartz volume and repeated elsewhere. He compiled a bibliography of Jewish scholarship for 1938 and 1939, the last two years of Jewish life in Europe. In his examination of the Jewish life that existed in Poland right before the Nazis came, he found that, in every area of learning, there was the kind of creativity that, if it had happened at another time, would have been remembered as the height of the culture. Rabbinic works were published in those two years in Poland that, had they been published a thousand years earlier, would have ranked with Maimonides. He felt toward the Bundists and the Zionists and the Polish poets and especially the rabbis a great respect, something beyond respect: an identification with his own world.

When Baron looked at America, he would note, "The American Jewish community is a boiling mess." (He didn't use exactly that word.) He would point out that it takes five hundred years for a new cultural center to define itself, though because culture moves faster in our age, it will take a little less time—perhaps a couple of hundred years. But he noted that the American Jewish community was a very young community. Most American Jews have been here, at most, a hundred years. And they brought with them the mentality of Eastern Europe, where they never lived as equals, where they lived under intense anti-Semitism. This community, he said, has enormous energy in a wide variety of fields. He intimated that some of that energy would dissipate into American

Salo W. Baron. Events Collection, 1965–83, Columbia University Archives and Columbiana Library, Columbia University in the City of New York.

society as a whole, some would be wasted, and many things would go amiss. But basically, he insisted that the community was engaged in redefining itself. Yes, there would be losses, enormous losses. And yet something would happen that would define *this* community as a great new center of Jewish history.

To summarize – though I have left out much that I intended to say and so many of his ideas that I intended to quote – there is a good, old-fashioned rabbinic term that comes to mind to define Baron: *bitachon* – faith, trust. There are in Baron's writing of Jewish history, with all his awareness of the losses and the tragedies, an enormous sympathy for the entire spectrum of Jewish creativity and a faith, a trust, that something would come of it. Trust that this community is not the end, but a fresh beginning. And what made it possible for Baron to believe this? Apart from the traditional reasons—this was the faith he was brought up on—what made it possible for him to believe? I think that, in the last analysis, it was because he himself was so personally the incandescent quintessence of the energy that Jewish history and Jewish learning, Jewish creativity, had stored up. He was all of Judaism in one person, a kind of pure energy, carrying forward the learning and the teaching of Jewish experience. He could not believe that the sources from which *he* had come, from which he had been created, could possibly have dried up. He believed that this kind of energy would continue.

Let me finish where I began, very personally. Many years ago, when Baron realized that he wasn't going to finish *A Social and Religious History of the Jews*, he and Jeannette sat me down and said, "You will, of course, finish it." I replied, "Professor Baron, you know that I don't have the learning, I don't have the energy. I simply don't know enough." He looked at me as if to say, "'I simply don't know enough' is an admission that you ought to work harder." So I refused. And until I started to prepare for this essay, I said to myself, "No way. Not ever. It just can't be done." Though I still know that it cannot be done, I have changed my mind to this degree: in his work Baron was saying something about modern Jewish experience that needs to be put together critically, to be argued with. I find myself, when reading him again, engaging in dialogue with him, perhaps engaging in a deeper dialogue because I am arguing with him as one argues in our tradition, on the margins of a volume of the Talmud. And so, if the Lord gives me strength, I will take this essay as the beginning of whatever I can do to redeem the promise that I never made. I shall write about Baron as a modern Jewish historian, making a serious attempt to understand modern Jewish history as he understood it and because I disagree with him in very serious matters. The subjects he raised, which he never was able to finish examining, deserve further exploration. I hope to be able to do so.

Baron occasionally quoted the Bible. Let me conclude by quoting the Bible as well. In Numbers, after the twelve spies went into the Holy Land, ten of them came back and said, despite the opposition of Joshua and Caleb, "The people are giants. They are much too great for us. They are beyond us." A number of us grew up in a generation in which the people we were privileged to study under were of the order of Baron and Lynn Thorndike of Columbia; of Harry A. Wolfson, under whom I spent a year at Harvard; of Gershom Scholem; and of Louis Ginzberg, Saul Lieberman, and Alexander Marx of the Jewish Theological Seminary. These were the giants of Jewish scholarship. The best contribution that those of us who are still around and knew them can make is to teach the next generations that a great scholar is not a figment of the *New York Times* Sunday magazine section. A great scholar belongs in the tradition of Maimonides, of Albo, of Joseph Karo, and of St. Thomas Aquinas and Dr. Johnson. A great scholar belongs in the tradition of those who understood and contemplated what knowledge says about human existence. Baron was one of the last of the giants. And the more I read of him, the more I realize that this man whom I could never persuade to attend *shul* remained, in the grand manner, a great rabbi.

The Material

The moon-stirred volume of ocean sighed
Coconut tanning oil and frozen custard.

Birch horses and dragons rode the merry-go-round.

A splinter of the herringbone cedar boardwalk
Might be teased from your finger with a steel
Needle purged of germs by a match's flame.

When the sliver was pulled out they held it
Up to your eyes, with bits of your flesh or blood
Stuck to it. Some doctors believe it helps
To see your tumor or gallbladder floating in a jar.

If Nana sewed a button on my shirt while I
Was wearing it, she made me chew a bit
Of the same cotton thread to keep the stitches
From piercing the precious tissues of my heart.

On the Day of Atonement she sat upstairs.

The shul was within sound of the ocean.

Across the street, Our Lady Star of the Sea
With the rumored mutable crackers and wine
Somewhere in its dark. Froth of Communion dresses.

Three round medallions filled the rainbow arc
Of our shul's jewel-colored Palladian
Window three stories tall, with three images:

The eight-branched lamp, the double tablets of law,
The Star of David – Study, Obedience and Pride?
Or blessedness at Home, in Heaven and the World?

Eight and Two and Six inscrutable
As the narcotic English translation my eye
Might swim to from the phonetic surf of Hebrew.
Meaning secreted itself in the urgent uncomprehended

Syllables the cantor sobbed,
In the building's eight miniature gilded minarets,
Terra cotta pilasters and three high double doors—
In the velvet and silver fittings
Of the Torah you kissed only by kissing the fringe
Of your tallis and reaching to press
The fringe to the cloaked scroll.

It flirted and hid itself in names, Sol Tepper,
Manny Horn, Isador Moss. Iossel, the ever-smiling "simple"
Concentration camp survivor they treated like a child—
Grinning, but his dark round eyes like pictures
Of the starved, the mutilated, orphans deprived of touch.

The same men called to the bima to pray by secret
Desert-names: Reuven ben Nachman, Moshe ben Yakov,
Yisrael ben Avraham, in wingtip shoes and neckties.

And with Nana upstairs Sophie Gorcey, Molly Joffe,
Suzy Diamond looking down from the balcony.

Nylons, hat feathers, double breasted suits.
Prescribed times to rise or sit or when those recently
Bereaved were supposed to leave the building
Or remain, or enter again through the three doors
Framed by four Ionic columns.

The church the synagogue the boardwalk all razed,
Merry-go-round carted off—temporary as gestures,
Icons expendable, less enduring than names.

Made things like garments. Means. Conduits,
Like the dark vaulted cylindrical tunnel that ran
Under Ocean Avenue between the pool at Chelsea Baths
And the beach, where people descended from the bright
Stucco pavilions into the dark round mouth
And then padded out onto the beach broiling in the sun:

Dim passageway from one blinding glare
Into a greater one, walkway invisible under the traffic,
Black damp mouth of the real, leading
From incomprehensible brightness to brightness.

—Robert Pinsky

JONATHAN D. SARNA

"Facing the New World"
What Portraits of Early American Jews Reveal and What They Obscure

Gilbert Stuart, Sarah Rivera Lopez (Mrs. Aaron Lopez) and Her Son Joshua Lopez, *1772/73. Oil on canvas, 26 × 21½ in. (66 × 54.6 cm). The Detroit Institute of Arts, Gift of Dexter M. Ferry, Jr. Photograph © The Detroit Institute of Arts.*

In 1997 The Jewish Museum presented *Facing the New World,* the finest exhibit ever assembled of early American Jewish portraits.[1] In thinking about the eighty-seven works displayed in the exhibition, I shall focus less on what these wonderful portraits reveal than on what they obscure. For what they obscure is Judaism; that is, the religious life of early American Jews. And this raises two questions: First, what do we know of the religious life of early American Jews? And second, why did early American Jews not include any sign of their religion in their portraits?

Early American Jewish religious life, from the eighteenth century on, revolved around the synagogue. Each major community had a synagogue, and it dominated the community's religious life—so much so that the synagogue and the community were one and the same. In New York, the most important of America's early Jewish communities, the synagogue was located in a small rented house on Mill Street, which is today South William Street. Known as the Jews' Synagogue or Shearith Israel, its official name was Kahal Kadosh She'arit Yisrael (Holy Congregation Remnant of Israel), and each of those Hebrew words was significant. Remnant of Israel—the synagogue's proper name—hinted at the promise of redemption. "I will surely gather the *remnant of Israel,*" the prophet Micah (Micah 2:12) had promised, and the Dutch rabbi Manasseh ben Israel believed that this gathering up might be imminent when Jews scattered to the four corners of the world. Early American Jews eagerly anticipated the coming of the messiah. They tried to calculate when he would arrive; they threw open their windows during thunderstorms to pray for his arrival; and some engaged in all-night prayer rituals designed to speed that arrival. Like many of their Protestant neighbors, they believed that better days were near at hand.[2] They looked forward to the ingathering of the exiles and the restoration of the Jews to the Land of Israel.

The congregation also considered itself to be a *kahal kadosh*, a holy community. In this, it closely resembled its Old and New World counterparts. It assumed responsibility for, and monopolized, all aspects of Jewish religious life: communal worship, dietary laws, life-cycle events, education, philanthropy, ties to Jews around the world, oversight of the cemetery and the ritual bath, even the baking of matzo and the distribution of Passover *haroset*. It saw itself, and was seen by others, as the representative body of the Jewish community. The congregation acted in the name of all area Jews, and the synagogue served as a place of meeting and gathering—a venue, as Abigaill Franks (whose portrait was in the exhibit) tells us, for exchanging "news and tatle [gossip]."[3]

The advantages of this all-encompassing kahal kadosh were, from a Jewish point of view, considerable. The synagogue-community proved a highly efficient means of meeting the needs of an outpost Jewish community. It promoted group solidarity and discipline. It evoked a sense of tradition as well as a feeling of kinship with similarly organized synagogue-communities throughout the Jewish world. And it enhanced the chances that even small clusters of Jews, remote from the wellsprings of Jewish learning, could survive from one generation to the next.

Looming large among the values espoused by the synagogue-community were tradition and deference. These two values had stood Sephardic Jews in good stead for generations and were considered essential to Jewish survival itself. At Shearith Israel, various prayers, including part of the prayer for the government, continued to be recited in Portuguese, the language of the original immigrants. The congregation's original minutes were likewise written in Portuguese, even though only a minority of the members understood that language and most spoke English in their day-to-day lives. Portuguese represented tradition; it was the language not only of the community's founders but also of what they liked to call the Portuguese Jewish "nation" scattered around the world. (Ladino, or Judeo-Spanish, written in Hebrew characters, was spoken mainly by the Sephardim of the Ottoman Empire.) In matters of worship, too, Shearith Israel closely conformed to the traditional *minhag* (ritual) as practiced by Portuguese Jews in Europe and the West Indies. Innovations were prohibited; "Our duty," Sephardic Jews in England (writing in Portuguese) once explained, is "to imitate our forefathers."[4] On a deeper level, Sephardic Jews believed, as did the Catholics among whom they had so long lived, that ritual could unite those whom life had dispersed. They wanted members of their nation to feel at home in any Sephardic synagogue anywhere in the world: the same liturgy, the same customs, even the same tunes.

Deference formed part of the Sephardic mind-set as well. Worshippers expected to submit to the officers and elders of the congregation, which was entirely lay dominated. As in most religious and political institutions of the day, power was vested in men of means. At Shearith Israel, governing authority rested in the hands of the *parnas* (president or warden), assisted by a small number of officers and elders who constituted the *mahamad*, or *adjunta* (standing committee). These were usually men of wealth and substance who took on the burden of communal leadership out of a sense of noblesse oblige. *Yehidim* (first-class members), generally men of status who materially supported the congregation, made most of the important decisions; they were the equivalent of communicants in colonial Protestant churches. The rest of the worshippers, including all the women, occupied seats at services but held no authority.

No Jewish religious authority of any kind in colonial America possessed sufficient status to challenge the authority of the laity. Neither Shearith Israel, nor any of the synagogues subsequently established before the Revolution, ever hired a *haham* (sage; the title given to a rabbi in the Sephardic community), nor did rabbis regularly grace American pulpits until 1840. Sermons, when they were delivered at all, were offered by visitors or by the officiating (unordained) reader. London's Sephardic synagogue had considered it "necessary and imperative . . . to have a Haham," and appointed one in 1664, just seven years after the congregation was founded, to "instruct us and teach the observance of the most Holy Law."[5] In America, the Jewish communities of Recife, Curaçao, Surinam, Barbados, and Jamaica all enjoyed the religious leadership of a haham at various times in the seventeenth and eighteenth centuries. In New York a dearth of members and funds partly explains why Shearith Israel did not follow suit; as late as 1750 the city's Jewish population did not exceed three hundred (sixty families). But the practice of local churches probably explains more. Only about a fourth of the Christian congregations in the province of New York enjoyed full-time pastors in 1750, and even the Anglicans failed to appoint a bishop to oversee their flock. The absence of a professional religious authority thus did not embarrass Jews in the eyes of their neighbors.

The ultimate authority available to the synagogue-community was the power of the *herem*, or excommunication, "the principal means of defining social deviance and of removing from the community wayward members whose actions and behavior offended its values."[6] The anathematized person lost all rights within the Jewish community and was treated as if he were dead. Synagogues threatened this punishment far more often than they actually invoked it, for its effectiveness in a society where Jews and Christians mixed freely was highly dubious, and there was always the danger that it would backfire and bring the whole Jewish community into disrepute. More commonly, therefore, punishments consisted of fines, denial of synagogue honors, and, most effective, threatened exclusion from the Jewish cemetery—punishments limited to the religious sphere and thus parallel to church forms of discipline.

What really sustained the colonial synagogue-community was not so much discipline as a consensus concerning the importance of maintaining Judaism and its central values. Shearith Israel's new Mill Street Synagogue, consecrated in 1730 and portrayed in the exhibit, reflected this consensus in its very architecture and design. Never before had North American Jews built (or even owned) a synagogue, so this was their first opportunity to shape the urban landscape. Since the completion of Trinity Church by the Anglicans in 1696, a slew of competing houses of worship had been built in New York City, including French, Dutch Reformed, Lutheran, and Presbyterian churches. These opulently designed buildings, with large spires and towers, transformed and sacralized the city's skyline and displayed the colonists' burgeoning material success for all to see.

Jews had likewise achieved material success (the house of the wealthy Jewish merchant Lewis M. Gomez, for example, was assessed at nearly ten times the value of the frame building that Shearith Israel had previously rented as its house of worship), but the new synagogue building as finally constructed favored tradition over external display. It focused on the interior of the synagogue, designed in classical Sephardic style, while keeping the exterior comparatively simple, on the scale of the modest New York churches and meetinghouses built by the persecuted Baptists and Quakers. In this, local Jews emulated the pattern of clandestine churches (*schuilkerken*) in early modern Europe and of London's Sephardic synagogue, Bevis Marks, completed in 1701. They also anticipated what the Jews of Newport, Rhode Island, would do when they completed their synagogue, Jeshuat Israel (now known as the Touro Synagogue), in 1763. All these houses of worship were disguised as domestic structures on the outside to distinguish them visually from the major community churches and avoid offending the majority faith. They projected an image of deference, offering neighbors the reassurance that Jews kept to themselves. In so doing, they reinforced for local Jews an important cultural lesson that cen-

Attributed to Gerardus Duyckinck, Jacob Franks, *c. 1735. Oil on canvas, 44 × 35 in. (111.8 × 88.9 cm). American Jewish Historical Society, Waltham, Massachusetts, and New York, Gift of Captain N. Taylor Phillips.*

turies of diaspora experience had repeatedly taught them: to practice great discretion on the outside, not drawing excessive attention to themselves, while glorying in their faith on the inside, where tradition reigned supreme.

That same idea, I think, is the key to understanding the early American Jewish portraits in the 1997 exhibit. They were designed to be gazed upon by outsiders who might visit Jewish homes. And they were painted by outsiders, early American artists who, whatever their artistic abilities, knew little of Judaism and Jewish life. Significant Jewish portrait artists appear in America only in the

Attributed to Gerardus Duyckinck, Phila Franks, *c. 1735. Oil on canvas, 46 × 36 in. (115 × 91.5 cm). American Jewish Historical Society, Waltham, Massachusetts, and New York, Gift of Captain N. Taylor Phillips.*

nineteenth century. The portraits in the exhibit discussed here — by what they conceal as much as by what they reveal — thus are evidence of the compartmentalization of colonial American Jewish life into Jewish and worldly domains. That distinction was unknown to medieval Jews, or, for that matter, to most European Jews of the day, but it was characteristic of American Judaism almost from the beginning. Colonial synagogue-communities did not tax commercial transactions, censor what Jews wrote on the outside, or punish members for lapses in individual or business morality, unlike synagogues in Amsterdam, London, and Recife, the Brazilian town from which New York's original colony of Jews migrated in 1654. Instead, like the neighboring churches, they confined their activities to the religious sphere, disciplining religiously wayward congregants with fines and loss of religious privileges but leaving commercial and civil disputes—even those that pitted one Jew against another—to the municipal authorities. Some Sephardic Jews went so far as to employ different names in each realm, recalling their former double identities as crypto-Jews. The renowned Newport merchant Aaron Lopez (1731–1782), for example, occasionally inscribed his business ledgers with his Portuguese baptismal name, Duarte. In the synagogue, he was always known as Aaron. In short, colonial Jews led bifurcated lives, complete with rules, institutions, and customs that kept synagogue life and general life distinct.

Complete compartmentalization, of course, was impossible. Central Jewish observances—the Sabbath, Jewish holy days, Jewish dietary laws—blurred the boundaries that the separation of realms sought so scrupulously to maintain, and engendered painful conflicts between the demands of Jewish law and the norms of the larger society in which Jews lived. Many of the individuals whose portraits are exhibited in *Facing the New World* experienced these conflicts, none more strongly than Jacob and Abigaill Franks upon the intermarriage of their daughter, Phila, in 1742, to the Huguenot merchant Oliver DeLancey. "I am now retired from Town and would from my Self," Abigaill wrote, describing her shock at the marriage. Abigaill withdrew from the city and in traditional Jewish fashion resolved never to see her daughter again, "nor Lett none of the Family Goe near her."[7]

Yet realities like intermarriage, as well as similar conflicts between Jewish norms and American life, unfortunate as colonial Jews found them to be, did not intrude upon their ideals, which is what their portraits represent. Indeed, in their portraits, colonial Jews displayed themselves as they wished themselves to be seen by their elite non-Jewish neighbors, which is why the portraits highlight Jews' status and class. The practice of Judaism, by contrast, was to them a private and intimate aspect of their lives. They hid it from those who portrayed them and shared it only with their fellow Jews, far from the artist's gaze.

Shirt

The back, the yoke, the yardage. Lapped seams,
The nearly invisible stitches along the collar
Turned in a sweatshop by Koreans or Malaysians

Gossiping over tea and noodles on their break
Or talking money or politics while one fitted
This armpiece with its overseam to the band

Of cuff I button at my wrist. The presser, the cutter,
The wringer, the mangle. The needle, the union,
The treadle, the bobbin. The code. The infamous blaze

At the Triangle Factory in nineteen-eleven.
One hundred and forty-six died in the flames
On the ninth floor, no hydrants, no fire escapes—

The witness in a building across the street
Who watched how a young man helped a girl to step
Up to the windowsill, then held her out

Away from the masonry wall and let her drop.
And then another. As if he were helping them up
To enter a streetcar, and not eternity.

A third before he dropped her put her arms
Around his neck and kissed him. Then he held
Her into space, and dropped her. Almost at once

He stepped up to the sill himself, his jacket flared
And fluttered up from his shirt as he came down,
Air filling up the legs of his gray trousers—

Like Hart Crane's Bedlamite, "shrill shirt ballooning."
Wonderful how the pattern matches perfectly
Across the placket and over the twin bar-tacked

Corners of both pockets, like a strict rhyme
Or a major chord. Prints, plaids, checks,
Houndstooth, Tattersall, Madras. The clan tartans

Invented by mill-owners inspired by the hoax of Ossian,
To control their savage Scottish workers, tamed
By a fabricated heraldry: MacGregor,

Bailey, MacMartin. The kilt, devised for workers
to wear among the dusty clattering looms.
Weavers, carders, spinners. The loader,

The docker, the navvy. The planter, the picker, the sorter
Sweating at her machine in a litter of cotton
As slaves in calico headrags sweated in fields:

George Herbert, your descendant is a Black
Lady in South Carolina, her name is Irma
And she inspected my shirt. Its color and fit

And feel and its clean smell have satisfied
both her and me. We have culled its cost and quality
Down to the buttons of simulated bone,

The buttonholes, the sizing, the facing, the characters
Printed in black on neckband and tail. The shape,
The label, the labor, the color, the shade. The shirt.

—Robert Pinsky

BARBARA KIRSHENBLATT-GIMBLETT

The Moral Sublime

Jewish Women and Philanthropy in Nineteenth-Century America

At the Fair

Scenes of sunny brightness,
Gleams of beauty rare,
Gems of dazzling splendor
At the Fair.

Eyes that sparkle merriment,
Smiles that banish care,
Voices sweet and tender
At the Fair.

Booths of varied grandeur,
Floating in the air,
Radiant Eastern visions
At the Fair.

Hearts that feel for sorrow,
Giving all a share,
Love's eternal treasures,
At the Fair.

Pocketbooks capacious,
Checks beyond compare,
Flourish all around you
At the Fair.

—*"Robin," in* Jewish Messenger,
December 13, 1895

The most powerful fund-raising tool during the nineteenth century in the United States was the charity fair. The biggest of these fairs, which were all organized by women, could raise in excess of a million dollars in a matter of weeks. This was a staggering sum for the period. No other method of fund-raising —not banquets, balls, or benefit performances, not subscriptions or appeals—produced so much money so quickly. Raising money for a good cause, the purpose of these fairs, was not all they achieved, however. These events did much more. They shaped public life and deliberately placed women at its center. And in addition their decline marked the shift from a focus on charity to one on philanthropy in American Jewish life.

Before the Civil War, individual groups organized fairs of modest scope and duration, known variously as church fairs, ladies' fairs, fancy fairs, charity fairs, and bazaars. These events, based on English models, had been popular in New

Cover of the Souvenir Book of the Fair in Aid of the Educational Alliance and Hebrew Technical Institute *(1895)*

England since the 1830s. They featured women's needlework as well as donated goods, refreshments, and various entertainments. Jewish charity fairs in the United States date from at least the 1850s. A reporter for the *Jewish Messenger* remembered attending "a bright Fair, even though it was of small dimensions, in 1859, which was held in a store on Broadway near 12th Street for the benefit of a society of the Portuguese Congregation."[1]

It was during the Civil War that the blockbuster fair was born. These fairs were known as sanitary fairs because they were prompted by the urgent need to address unsanitary medical conditions on the battlefield. During the Civil War more men were dying in infirmaries than on the battlefield because of unsanitary conditions, inadequate medical supplies, and understaffing of infirmaries. Compassion for the men on the field and for the women and children they left behind, often without support, prompted women to lobby the government to form the United States Sanitary Commission, which they then helped fund by raising millions of dollars through sanitary fairs across the country. These spectacular events wedded the purposes and style of the venerable ladies' fairs with aspects of three contemporaneous developments: world's fairs, department stores, and museums.

Like world's fairs (the first was held in London's Crystal Palace in 1851; New York hosted its own Crystal Palace in 1853), the sanitary fairs, which were organized by existing voluntary associations or by specially created committees, encouraged broad national and international participation. Individual states as well as nations were represented at the sanitary fairs. Britain, for example, showed support for the Sanitary Commission's efforts to care for sufferers on both sides of the Civil War by displaying its flag at the Metropolitan Fair, a sanitary fair held in Manhattan in 1864. Even the exhibits and entertainments at sanitary fairs owed something to world's fairs, which were famous for their reconstructions of historical settings and presentations of exotic cultures. Thus, the Metropolitan Fair featured the Indian Department, which included not only American Indian "relics" but also the performance of "war dances."[2] Like the department store (the first was Paris's Bon Marché in 1852), sanitary fairs were organized into departments based on types of goods, and they were designed to make a grand impression, offering booths full of merchandise along with the refreshments, exhibitions, and entertainment. Sanitary fairs even served as temporary museums. Indeed, the excitement generated by the art exhibition at the 1864 Metropolitan Fair prompted New Yorkers to call for the establishment of a civic art museum, and resulted in the founding of The Metropolitan Museum of Art in 1870.

The early Jewish fairs were relatively small, and generally organized by a single institution. In an 1857 letter, the philanthropist Rebecca Gratz refers to such a fair for the Jewish Foster Home in Philadelphia, an institution that had been established in 1855 at her urging. In contrast, the enormous fairs of the post–Civil War period required the joint efforts of most if not all the major congregations, lodges, charities, hospitals, and educational institutions of the Jewish community. The biggest of them all was the Fair in Aid of the Educational Alliance and Hebrew Technical Institute, held at Madison Square Garden in New York in 1895. The *Jewish Messenger* compared this fair with earlier ones: "New York Israel has seen plenty of fairs—from the old-time bazaar in the forgotten Allemania Hall to the brilliant scene in the Armory at 36th street and Broadway; from the rich setting at the Brunswick to the splendors of the Rink at 60th street and Boulevard; or even the Madison Square Garden itself, when benevolent society, hospital, free school, home, and the rest were successively benefited. But never has there been a fair so brilliant, beautiful, and extensive."[3]

The cooperation of so many Jewish organizations in one joint venture was evidence of the community's solidarity, despite its differences. This "miracle," which was said to surpass even those recounted at the Passover seder, showed "how Jews can unite, whether they say long prayers, short prayers, or no printed prayers at all, to help the good cause." While the Educational Alliance fair was particularly ambitious, it was not alone in claiming to be the biggest and the best—and the most successful at rallying the Jewish community as a whole. The 1870 fair in aid of the Hebrew Benevolent and Orphan Asylum Society and Mount Sinai Hospital was expected to eclipse "not only all previous efforts made in the Jewish community, but every Fair held by any denomination in aid of any object ever held in this city—with the single exception of the Grand Sanitary Fair of 1864."[4]

Historians generally mention these fairs only in passing, as examples of methods used by women to raise money for various causes. They find the charitable organizations themselves more important than the fund-raising methods these organizations used, although important work has been done on the history of charitable Jewish women, especially German Jewish women, in the nineteenth century.[5] During this period, philanthropy played a crucial role in the way German Jews, who had arrived in significant numbers earlier than Eastern European Jews and were well established, related to the more recent immigrants. Studies of charity fairs tend to focus on Christian (largely Protestant) fairs.[6] Much, however, can be learned from a close examination of charity fairs in their own right and from Jewish fairs in particular.

Jewish charity fairs offer a living picture—a panorama—of the Jewish community as it understood itself and wanted to be seen. Part snapshot and part formal portrait, the fairs were exercises in self-definition as well as image management. They were also agencies of solidarity and an early experiment in community-wide action. New York's burgeoning and diversified Jewish community was characterized by a proliferation of associations, institutions, and congregations that marked divisions based on class, gender, age, place of origin, religious ideology, and occupation. Their friendly and not-so-friendly rivalries were frequently noted.

New York's Jews, whose numbers increased tenfold between 1840 and 1860, were exceptional in their proclivity toward organization. According to the historian Hasia Diner, "Between 1848 and 1860, when Jews made up somewhere between two and five percent of the city's total population, they supported more than ninety-three philanthropic associations. The rest of the city maintained only ninety-six similar institutions." Yet New York's Jews, the largest Jewish community in the United States, had no central communal organization until a *kehillah* was established in 1908. And that, according to Arthur A. Goren, was an "experiment," which lasted only until 1922.[7] As the Jewish community became larger and more diverse with the influx of Eastern European Jews through the 1880s, it became more urgent to coordinate charitable activity and Jewish organizational life more generally.

Jewish communal life was made complex by fissures, splits, and mergers. The fairs created an opportunity, ephemeral as it might have been, for a large number of Jews who were otherwise attached to competing organizations to act in concert, find strength in numbers, and see themselves as a whole, as well as for newly merged organizations to consolidate their forces.

Allowing Jews to express solidarity without requiring consensus on many issues, these fairs spoke to the prosperity, self-sufficiency, and public spirit of the Jewish community. Sympathetic observers such as the photographer Jacob Riis, who was duly impressed with the 1895 Educational Alliance fair, had nothing but praise for Jewish communal self-sufficiency: "There was the great fair, so fresh in the public mind, at which a fortune was realized for the Jewish charities of the city. It is more than 240 years since the Jews were first admitted, by special license, as it were, to the New Netherlands, on the express condition that 'the poor among them should not become a burden to the company or the community, but be supported by their own nation,' and most loyally have they kept the compact that long since ceased to have force to bind. Their poor are not, and never were, a burden upon the community."[8] Far from being a burden on society, Jews were positively public-spirited. Their hospitals and technical schools were open to everyone, regardless of creed.

Women were active organizers of these events, which bore the imprint of their sensibility, and their presence was perhaps the greatest attraction the fairs offered. Beautifully outfitted women appearing en masse in public created a brilliant spectacle, as male reporters of the period were fond of noting. Unusually inclusive, these events attracted men, women, and children; rich and poor; Jews and Christians. They offered a model of what an all-embracing public sphere might look like, although the fairs were not without their exclusions, divisions, and hierarchies.

Perhaps most important, the act of public assembly—Jews coming together in public, with great style, for a good cause—was taken as an important expression of Jewishness as well as the quintessence of what it meant to be American. At the opening ceremonies of the Educational Alliance fair, New York mayor William L. Strong quoted a "well-known Jewess of New York City," who informed girls and boys that if they were "good Jews and Jewesses," they would be "good American citizens."[9] In a word, these gatherings modeled how to be Jewish and American at the same time.

The Sanitary Fairs

The immediate model for the Jewish fairs that were held across the country during and after the Civil War was the sanitary fair. These became so popular that *Our Daily Fair*, the newspaper published daily at the 1864 Philadelphia Sanitary Fair, could refer to "the fair movement in the United States" and trace its history "in other countries and former wars," including the French Revolution, the Prussian uprising against the French in 1813, and the revolutionary movements in Europe in 1848. But, *Our Daily Fair* continued, despite the popular enthusiasm and patriotism they expressed, these earlier fairs had been "short-lived and spasmodic" in comparison with American sanitary fairs.[10]

During the Civil War, Jewish women's organizations redirected their efforts to wartime needs by collecting supplies, providing personal services, or sending the proceeds of their fund-raising efforts to the Sanitary Commission. Jewish women also formed new organizations expressly for wartime purposes. Some of these women and their organizations found that participation in the large metropolitan sanitary fairs offered them an unparalleled opportunity to demonstrate their patriotism by taking part in a spectacular local event with high national visibility. In New York, the organizers of the 1864 Metropolitan Fair included Jewish representatives on the various committees, "undoubtedly to assure the cooperation of all the Jewish organizations."[11] Jewish participation in these activities was a demonstration of patriotism and good citizenship that allowed Jews to show that they were not parochial.

Two principles governed the organization of the fairs. First, by arranging merchandise according to category, fair organizers emulated the rational plan of the department store. Indeed, these fairs operated as temporary department stores. Second, organizations were allowed to open their own booths. At the sanitary fair in Cincinnati in 1863, the Jewish community set up four stands, "one each by the Allemania Club, the Phoenix, a group calling themselves the 'Independent Ladies,' and the Broadway Synagogue." The Jewish stands were estimated to have earned about a third of the proceeds generated by the fair. However, Jews were not in accord on the question of group participation. Some felt that they should participate as citizens and should not label "Jewish participation as Jewish." Nor did they want to be the only ones to establish "denominational stands," an option sometimes exercised by other religious groups.[12]

The sanitary fairs built on the custom of charging admission to specially organized art exhibitions. Such exhibitions were a major attraction in cities that did not yet have an art museum and therefore depended on private collectors to open their treasures to the public for a good cause. Jewish art collectors were prominent in this endeavor. At the Metropolitan Fair, August Belmont was one of two collectors to exhibit his private art collection.[13] Belmont, né Schoenberg, was a German Jew by birth, and a banker who represented the Rothschilds' interests in the United States. He had entered New York society by marrying the daughter of Commodore Perry and converting to Christianity.

The sanitary fairs were covered in detail by the Jewish press, which provided a virtual guided tour of the highlights, among them the art. The *Jewish Messenger*, for example, recommended the art exhibition at the Metropolitan Fair to "those who never have been among the wondering visitors to the Louvre or the Munich Gallery," and went on to say that "the Gallery at the 14th Street building will compare more than favorably" to the painting and statuary at the Crystal Palace.[14] Such comments indicate the degree to which world's fairs were a point of reference for the sanitary fairs.

Above all, fairs offered women a way to appear in public. As an observer complained in 1864, the places that respectable American women could visit were limited: "There is one thing that always strikes us with wonder in the amusement world of New York, which is the want of matinees or afternoon entertainments. There are thousands of ladies and children, those who perhaps have not attendants even for evening amusements, who would be glad to patronize an afternoon performance if they had reliance on its perfect order and respectability. These are confined to the Museum, the Stereopticon and the Menagerie. Why some of our first-class theatres should not give an occasional matinee we do not know. Certainly there can be no better time for the experiment than during the Sanitary Fair, when the city will be full of strangers only in for the day, or citizens out for a day's pleasure."[15] In no small measure, the fairs addressed the need for a public social place in which women would be comfortable.

The apparent frivolity of these events, according to Beverly Gordon, was carefully staged by the women who organized them to display "the powerful playing at being powerless." These women worked their wonders as if by magic in the fairyland they deliberately contrived. They were sometimes faulted for tiring of "the daily routine of amateur shop keeping and dickering" and for sending their "clerks and subordinates" to fill in for them. But for the most part their efforts to organize and run these events, even when hidden behind an aura of frivolity, were arduous.[16] The illusion was cultivated and strategic, and it made the work of entrepreneurial women less threatening.

Terms like *fairyland* and *spectacle* indicate the appreciation of these fairs as an art form in their own right, a point that Gordon rightly emphasizes. Indeed, so dizzying was the impression they gave that one observer referred to the sanitary fair as the "Insanity Fair," while others spoke of fair mania. Some were concerned because the fairs were distracting women from the home production of clothing and food and from gathering supplies for the troops; money generated by the fair had to make up the shortfall in material goods.[17] For this and other reasons, the fairs were not as effective economically as they might have been.

The participation of Jewish women in sanitary fairs and other fund-raising efforts for the Sanitary Commission was a point of considerable pride, and lessons learned from the sanitary fairs were directly applied to the Jewish fairs. In anticipation of the 1870 fair to aid the Hebrew Benevolent and Orphan Asylum Society and Mount Sinai Hospital, the *Jewish Messenger* recommended "the plan pursued at the great Sanitary Fair of 1863 [*sic*] – the hall being divided into various sections and every table representing a distinct branch of trade," and insisted that "Our Fair could not have a better model than the great Sanitary Fair of 1863," which was praised for its systematic plan and a series of features that were to become standard at charity fairs.[18] The *Jewish Messenger* declared that in "picturesque appearance, elegance and perfection of detail, and substantial promise," the 1870 fair would "compare favorably with the most notable Bazaars our country has witnessed – not alone in pecuniary results, but in character as spectacle." A reporter gushed: "A more lovely spectacle can scarcely be imagined – glowing with bright colors, brilliant with light, gay and glorious in the noble assemblage of 'fair women and brave men.'" With those words he captured the moral sublime.[19] What better context for Jews – especially Jewish women – to appear in public, as Jews?

The Jewish Fairs

> *Tsey u-l'mad:* go and learn, ye that are in the metropolis;
> See for yourselves what is going on, what there is for sale,
> and how beautifully it is sold by fair women.
> – "The Fair in Progress," *American Hebrew*, December 13, 1895

During the second half of the nineteenth century, American Jewish women were the impresarios of some of the largest philanthropic social events in their communities. In conceiving, organizing, and managing these events, they not only raised large amounts of money in a very short time; they also helped create the public culture of their communities. A round of philanthropic activities gave form to Jewish social life—from the Purim balls and Hanukkah pageants popular during the latter half of the nineteenth century, both largely organized by men, to the Purim kettledrums (a pun on *tea kettle* and *drum* that refers to a noisy tea) and charity fairs, which were mainly in the hands of women.

Among German Jews, holding social events with charitable objectives became an important way of observing the Jewish holidays. Families rented boxes at opera houses where Purim balls were held, and received visitors there instead of at home. Special Purim quadrilles were composed for the occasion.[20] One member of the Purim Association used the term "social Judaism" for these events, which suggests the significance of Jewish association and sociability in public as an expression of Jewishness at this time. As many Jewish holiday celebrations moved out of the house and into public places—armories, opera houses, music academies, restaurants, and Masonic halls—the Jewish holiday calendar converged with social seasons and shopping cycles. Nowhere was this more clear than in the annual charity fairs held just before Christmas.[21] For Jews these fairs were a response to the December dilemma—specifically, the issue of how to deal with Christmas, and their anxieties about declining interest in Hanukkah. Timed to take advantage of the Christmas shopping season, the Jewish events were concerned less with "copying" the Gentiles, who also held charity fairs at this time, and more with using the form of the charity fair for Jewish ends.

Fairs like the one mounted to raise money for the Educational Alliance and Hebrew Technical Institute in 1895 became even larger, more sophisticated, and more professional in their management than those of the preceding two decades, as did the philanthropic organizations they supported. Those organizations faced new challenges during the Progressive Era, in particular the influx of Eastern European Jewish immigrants, who were ready targets for the Christian missionary movement. To protect them, established Jews organized their own "missions" in the form of Jewish vocational and technical schools that would not only teach trades but also socialize the newest arrivals into American and American Jewish life. The reorganization and consolidation of Jewish institutions of this period can be seen from the history of the Educational Alliance and the Hebrew Technical Institute.[22]

The Educational Alliance was created by the Hebrew Free School Association (founded in 1864), the Young Men's Hebrew Association (founded in 1874), and the Aguilar Free Library (founded in 1886). In 1889 the three groups organized a fair that raised about $125,000 for a new building. They formed a corporation, the Educational Alliance, to handle the money, oversee the building's construction, and manage it after it was occupied. The building for the new entity, which was known as the Hebrew Institute, opened its doors in 1891.[23] When the YMHA could not meet its financial obligations and withdrew, the remaining groups reorganized in 1893 and became a membership society. This reorganization was spearheaded by Isidor Straus, the department store magnate and congressman, who became president of the Educational Alliance.[24] The Hebrew Technical Institute (founded in 1883) grew out of the Hebrew Benevolent and Orphan Asylum Society (founded in 1822), the Hebrew Free School Association, and the United Hebrew Charities (founded in 1874).

The 1895 Fair in Aid of the Educational Alliance and Hebrew Technical Institute—the press referred to it generically as the Hebrew Fair, or the Great Hebrew Fair, or, more specifically, the Education Fair—was dedicated to raising money to pay off the mortgage on the Hebrew Institute building and cover other debts. In part because it is so well documented, this fair rewards close examination. Coming at the end of the period of fair mania, but organized with excessively high hopes, it also holds clues as to why such events went out of fashion. Like the earlier fairs, the Educational Alliance fair was praised as evidence of the "unanimity with which the entire Jewish community makes the cause of any one organization, when called upon to do so, its own," in the words of Isidor Straus. As he and others emphasized, the cause in question marked a shift in the culture of benevolence from charity (ameliorating misery) to philanthropy (preventing need) through education. As *The American Hebrew* explained, "It was not charity but philanthropy that animated the activity in preparing for the Fair," the proceeds of which would aid the students of the Educational Alliance and Hebrew Technical Institute "in becoming useful citizens, well-beloved by their Gentile neighbors and truly a credit to the Jewish race."[25]

Abram S. Hewitt, an industrialist, congressman, and former mayor of New York City, spoke at the opening. Taking the fair as evidence of the success of American democracy, he declared that only in America, in a "free land, where distinctions of birth, race and religion have no place in the economy of government," could Jewish people come together "in such numbers, in such wealth, and in such beauty." Indeed, Jewish success was "the greatest tribute to American institutions," for it offered proof of "the American principles of freedom." The fair, he continued, showed what Jews could do when they were free: "Of all the races in the world, they understand the meaning of self-help best," thanks to two thousand years of experience. To the "Jew baiter" he urged, "Come see!" The *Souvenir Book of the Fair in Aid of the Educational Alliance and Hebrew Technical Institute* featured a facsimile of the 1790 letter from George Washington to the Jews of Newport, Rhode Island, in which he lauded the new nation as the home of "liberty of consciousness and immunities of citizenship," specifically citing "the children of the stock of Abraham" as a kind of test case.[26]

The Educational Alliance fair departed from earlier fairs in ways that mark changes in American and American Jewish life and that can be seen in the fair's artistic ambitions and business practices.[27] Fairs generally opened with a grand ceremony and ended with an auction, announcements of the winners of contests, and a ball. Many of these elements were to be found at the Educational Alliance fair to be sure, but with a difference. The opening ceremonies, for example, were noteworthy for being exceptionally short, less than half an hour, as if to say: "Enough with the formalities. Get on with the shopping!" Given the enormous and impatient crowd, the speeches would have been difficult to hear in any case.

The fair also differed in its design. Departing from the eclectic look of many earlier fairs, where women designed and decorated their own stands as they pleased, the Educational Alliance fair was modeled on the unified look pioneered by department stores. Gathering many kinds of merchandise under one roof, department stores used design to create a coherent corporate image; this was in keeping with the era's tendency toward corporatization, of which the Educational Alliance was itself an example. The fair's unified look was accomplished by the department store magnates who administered it.[28]

Whereas women had been in charge of most of the earlier charity fairs, here their role was to manage individual booths and particular attractions, such as the art gallery. Mrs. William Einstein (née Hannah Bachman), who was active in charitable causes (and is remembered for her progressive views on the welfare of widowed and deserted mothers and their children), was in charge of the art exhibition. The display of 150 pictures, valued at $400,000, was celebrated as "superior to any loan exhibition seen at any other fair," and taken as indicative of Jewish appreciation and patronage of the arts. In his president's report for 1895, Isidor Straus wrote, "Too much cannot be said in praise of the ladies who participated in [the fair], and I trust that I may not be accused of invidious partiality when I ascribe our success largely to their zeal, energy, and devoted interest."[29] Everyone knew that women were essential to the success of the event (and that events like these were women's events), from organizing and managing the individual booths to using their charms to extract money from the visitors. Nonetheless, at this fair, men were decidedly at the helm, as they were in the two institutions that would benefit most from the fair—an arrangement that was not without its tensions. Just a year earlier, there had been an incident at the Educational Alliance in which trustee Nathan Straus, a brother of

Isidor Straus, prevented women from holding an anti-Tammany meeting in the building. The press took the disagreement as an indication that he "was evidently afraid of the work that the women may do in the Hebrew quarters of the city."[30]

Women's participation was thus contained within the unified plan created by the fourteen (or eighteen—the figure varies) professional architects commissioned to design the fair. The illustrations in the *Souvenir Book*, which had been published before the fair opened, reflect what they had in mind. The effect was feminine, so much so that one reporter was prompted to write as if a woman had dreamed up the design: "The octagon-shaped edifices in the centre were surely the beauteous dream of a chaste mind, so dainty with white and gold they were. Graceful pyramids of some fairy-like fabric rose above them to the apex of the roof, where bannerets of alternate white and golden gauze veiled the enormous girders of the building. At the flower stand the pillars were bound with smilax, so as to relieve the eye, which almost tired of the glitter of ivory and gold."[31] These structures, the center of attraction in the middle of the large hall, were dedicated to flower and candy sales, which were expected to bring in the largest revenues—and did. Candy sales accounted for $20,075 and flowers for $8,401.

The other stands were described as "gorgeously decorated in silk and stuffs of brilliant hue, with roofs of evergreens, after the manner of the symbolical booths used by the children of Israel" for Sukkoth, with the foliage supported on "Corinthian columns" like the ones found in the octagonal edifices. In this way, Jewish meanings were discreetly read into otherwise neutral materials such as evergreens, which were a standard feature at these events. But explicitly Jewish symbols were also to be found. Thus: "Around about the limits of the arena were built a range of twenty copartments [*sic*] decorated in red and festooned in various rich colors, each booth being divided from its neighbor by a golden shield bearing the noble device of 'the Lion of Judah.' Spears upheld the canopies at regular intervals, reminding the observer of the glorious days of the Maccabees." And: "At the end of the vast hall, opposite the main entrance was a row of columns, each one bearing a golden globe, grand souvenir of the Temple of Solomon."[32]

The total effect was not only a "scene of Oriental splendor" that would "rival what has been depicted by the authors of 'The Arabian Nights,'" but also one of unified vision and efficient management. The fair was praised in prose and verse for running "as smoothly as a first-class business." After the initial chaos of the opening crowds, it was also lauded for being "brilliant and orderly," both artistically and financially. This effect extended to the crowd, which was a

Candy stand, illustration from the Souvenir Book of the Fair in Aid of the Educational Alliance and Hebrew Technical Institute *(1895)*

spectacle in its own right, the dresses of the women, "in costly fabrics of every hue of the rainbow" set off against the dark clothing of the men.[33] Indeed, the crowd was the main attraction, as dignitaries like Abram S. Hewitt were quick to note from their privileged place in the gallery overlooking the arena.

From below the experience was quite different. Variously figured as a "solid phalanx," an "army of charity," a "wondrous scene of animated traffic, well punctuated by innocent flirtations," the crowd was so enormous that "one was carried along in the swim, as it were; swift locomotion toward any fixed point was impracticable."[34] The contrast with the more sinister characterizations of the threatening masses of the Lower East Side, the beneficiaries of the fair, could not be more striking.

Flower stand, illustration from the Souvenir Book of the Fair in Aid of the Educational Alliance and Hebrew Technical Institute *(1895)*

Charity fairs were predicated on a gift economy that women in particular understood. The Education Alliance fair, in contrast, was run like a business. At the helm of the Fair Association were Isidor Straus as president and Joseph B. Bloomingdale, as one of the vice presidents. These businessmen ensured that the style and discipline of the department store prevailed. As already noted, professional architects created a unified design for the fair and all transactions were conducted with an organized decorum. There was to be "no raffling, no selling of chances," according to the advertisements for the fair, although both actually did occur, as did auctions. The *New York Times*, which covered the fair extensively, declared that the methods would be "entirely different" from the usual. There would be no "buttonholing": "The army of young ladies will not wander about the auditorium persisting in the visitors buying chances; they will be found occupying positions behind the counters of the different booths and performing the duties of saleswomen. They will take pleasure in displaying such goods as the purchaser wishes to examine." Prices would be considerably below market rates and lots of bargains would be found. Contests would be conducted so as to "avoid any unpleasantness on the part of the visitors."[35]

In a word: "The projectors of this enterprise have simply converted Madison Square Garden into the largest [department] store in New-York for the time being," and all the proceeds would go to a good cause. One reporter noted that the favorite stands, which were crowded by lines of purchasers, "resembled bargain counters at department stores." With expenses reduced, an estimated $200,000 worth of stock donated (not only by Jews), and an estimated 1,000-to-1,500-person volunteer staff, the gross income, projected at $250,000, would be nearly all profit. Admission was twenty-five cents; a dollar for a season ticket. In fact, gross revenues fell far short of the goal, coming in at $165,109. The net was $142,570.01 to the penny. For a fair that was celebrated as "the largest Fair that the Jews of the city have given," this was a sign of its waning power as a fund-raising instrument. Twenty-five years earlier, in 1870, the fair held on behalf of the Hebrew Benevolent and Orphan Asylum Society and Mount Sinai Hospital had netted nearly as much, $140,000, an astonishing sum for the time. The 1886 fair for the Montefiore Home for Chronic Invalids, which raised the record sum of $175,000, could not be topped a decade later by the Educational Alliance fair.[36]

As for the sales force, these middle-class and well-to-do women were described as seductive, prying every penny from the pockets of smitten gentlemen by means of their charm and beauty. At the same time, they were described, tongue in cheek, as "Amazons . . . versed in the science of extraction," Robin Hoods, or highway robbers: "The women who worked for this occasion as vendors of votes for the many contests, had a difficult task getting at their victims. But their badges were accepted by the crowd as tokens of special privileges, and their unceremonious rushes were taken good-naturedly. Many a watch chain was torn in two and many a ribbon and piece of lace damaged by the rush of this army of handsome and active women, who had but one object in view—of getting at the visitors' exchequer"; "It was useless on the part of the victim to resort to subterfuge or excuse. . . . It was simply a metaphorical case of 'Hands up!' Many an old Western frontiersman was, for the time, carried back to the days when his wealth was taken from him by bold highwaymen."[37]

Even children were enlisted in the sales force on one Friday afternoon. The fair was described as "a veritable Lillyput Levée with the host of boys and girls as salespeople and shoppers, with rosy cheeks and wide-open eyes, bustling about and diffusing an atmosphere of radiant enjoyment."[38] Ironically, these are the activities that generated funds for an organization whose raison d'être was to train Jewish youth in so-called productive occupations—trades and industries—so that they would not revert to the traditional Jewish occupations of peddling and shopkeeping.

Strategically timed, these "festivals of consumption," to use Daniel Boorstin's apposite phrase, arrived at the height of the charity and the shopping seasons, which converged just before Christmas and coincided with the "winter festival of the Jews." References to the Jewish holiday could be found at the Educational Alliance fair, where "Chanuka lights were burned in the Y.M.H.A. Booth." For the children who attended, the fair itself was "a monster Hanukkah festival," in stark contrast with the way holidays were depicted by the German Jewish artist Moritz Daniel Oppenheim in his nostalgic, domestic "Scenes from Jewish Life," which "sold like hot-cakes." *The American Hebrew* printed an admonishing editorial alongside its coverage of the fair to the effect that children should be encouraged to celebrate Hanukkah so "the Christian celebration of their Gentile friends will have less attraction for them." Indeed, coming before or at the same time as Hanukkah, these fairs gave the holiday, which as early as the 1870s was "rapidly falling into disuse," a needed push.[39]

The business approach to the sale of goods in department store fashion did not eliminate what was most distinctive about these fairs, namely, their gift economy and spectacular displays of compassion, charity, and philanthropy. The fairs' gift economy reversed the logic that governed business. At the fairs merchants gave goods away and sellers did not keep the money they earned. People were encouraged to speculate in the irrational sphere of raffles, lotteries, and fortune-telling. Legitimizing the crime of vote-buying, they paid to vote and to vote as many times as they wished, whether for the most popular dentist or for the most popular little girl. They were encouraged to have their fortunes read by beautiful young women dressed in fantastic Gypsy costumes.

This economy depended literally on gifts, whether outright donations of cash, fancy goods, and food made by women expressly for the fair, volunteered services, or a variety of standard fair features that combined many of these elements. These included the post office, contests, raffles, lotteries, restaurants, and fair publications, among others. In 1888 Jewish women in Denver organized a fair for the synagogue's building fund, ran a profitable restaurant at the event, and published *The Fair Cook Book* to capitalize on its success. The *Souvenir Book* of the Educational Alliance fair was praised as one of the most lavish of its kind, featuring illustrated histories of the participating organizations. *The*

FAIR, 1895.

POST OFFICE.

Miss ANNETTA KOHN, Chairman.

Miss BEULA F. EINSTEIN,
Miss AMELIA EINSTEIN,
Miss ROSE KAUFMAN,
Miss HILDA STICH,
Miss LUCILLE MENKEN,
Miss AIMEE HEAVENRICH,
Miss DAISY HEAVENRICH,
Miss VIOLA KAUFMAN,
Miss LINDA STEINBERGER,
Miss CLAIRE LOWENSTEIN,
Miss IRENE LOWENSTEIN,
Miss BLANCHE VOGEL,
Miss BELLE ANSBACHER,
Miss MAUDE MINTZER,
Miss BERTHA SEISEL,
Miss TESSA CLARKE.

Page from the Souvenir Book of the Fair in Aid of the Educational Alliance and Hebrew Technical Institute *(1895) listing the young women of the fair's "post office" who delivered love messages on the fair floor*

Fair Journal, which appeared daily, provided "the latest news and gossip, with some solid reading."[40]

The "post office" consisted of lovely young women delivering love messages on the fair floor. The Educational Alliance fair, emulating the sanitary fairs, managed to persuade United States Postmaster-General Wilson to make it "a regular sub-station." He commissioned Annette Kohn as postmistress, "allowing her the privilege of appointing fifteen young lady carriers," who were dressed in letter-carrier uniforms. The post office raised $807 in a method described by *The American Hebrew:* "Victims" were "run, or rather rushed, by beautiful maidens. Their impetuous manner of forcing an envelope into your hand sealed and stamped, and the rest of the post-official *modus operandi,* made them for the time being the loveliest creatures in the vast encampment" of thirty-eight booths.[41] Such forward behavior on the part of young women, characterized in several accounts as Amazons, was countenanced at the fair, which provided a public space, however temporary, for female assertiveness.

The voting contests were often coordinated with "special days," a standard world's fair tactic for recruiting special constituencies. At the Educational Alliance fair, there were voting contests "for the most charitable organization, temple, regiment, president of an institution (charitable), and popular judge, not counting for the most popular college."[42] December 12 was Military Day, and the entire National Guard was expected to attend and vote for its favorite regiment; the prize was a silk regimental flag that had been donated by Jackson's, the dry goods house. Other prizes included a grandfather clock, a gold and silver clock, a banner, and a gavel.

The various constituencies were given the opportunity to participate in spectacles of compassion. These included the display of the beneficiaries of the charity in bands and choruses, as well as ceremonies of benevolence such as the dispensing of treats, toys, tours, and rides. Thus, the children of the Jewish Orphan Asylum and the Brightside Day Nursery were given a tour of the Educational Alliance fair and served a banquet in the dining hall. The children were also treated to popcorn, chocolate, and cake, and each child was presented with a doll. The band of the Hebrew Orphan Asylum, made up entirely of boys under the age of fourteen, led a delegation from the Mount Neboh lodge on a march through the building and, during the evening, shared the bandstand with the Victor Herbert Orchestra. Three hundred pupils from the Hebrew Free School sang, in several choruses.[43] Such performances not only allowed the institutions responsible for the children to promote themselves; they also provided a way to structure the massive presence of children and intensify the spectacle of compassion by placing the most tender beneficiaries at center stage and inviting them to perform for the beneficence that had been bestowed upon them. At the fair the children saw themselves being seen even as they witnessed their benefactors on display.

A reporter from *The American Hebrew* noted that the greatest crowd was gathered around the boys at work at the Hebrew Technical Institute booths. "The handiwork of these clever boys was given to spectators," he continued, "and the demand for souvenirs has far exceeded the supply." The reporter named the boys running the machines, provided their biographies, and celebrated their skills. Each one was a potential Horatio Alger. These live displays were indebted to a century of industrial fairs as well as to the "machinery halls" of world's fairs. They also demonstrated the transformation of spectacles of charity into demonstrations of philanthropy. As *The American Hebrew* explained, the difference between charity and philanthropy, as evidenced at the fair, was that instead of shutting out "by a small donation, misery from sight," the fair provided "the younger generation of our people and even succeeding generations with what the foresight of our communal leaders demonstrated would aid them in becoming useful citizens."[44]

An astonishing feature of the mammoth fairs—indeed, what made them possible at all, their gift economy notwithstanding—was their relation to the burgeoning consumer culture of the period. Before the Civil War, the wealthy had difficulty finding goods, and the Anglo-American elite eschewed public celebrations, preferring to retreat to their homes. Fancy fairs, as their name indicates, featured fancy needlework and other items made by the women who ran the fairs. After the Civil War consumer culture blossomed, and these fairs offered an outlet for the overstock of stores and for the contents of overstuffed closets. Fairs became an important way station in the "social life of things"; they offered things an afterlife by reversing the direction of their flow.[45] Sent back into the world, these possessions fell into the hands and homes of a second and third round of consumers. As promoters of redemptive shopping, women and their fairs were partners in the circulation of wealth and in the redistribution of goods through the irrational gift economy of the fair.

By the end of the century, the fairs had become so big, so arduous to run, and also so predictable that charitable organizations became leery of using them to raise money. Some felt that the very idea of the fair was worn out. By the 1930s these affairs had dwindled into the small ventures organized by local schools, churches, and synagogues that are familiar today.

Several factors were at work in the decline of the fairs. Perhaps most important was the professionalization of philanthropy, a change not only in how money was raised but also in the very nature of philanthropic work, which was to proceed on a more rational, if not scientific, basis.[46] Women who might earlier have made fancywork, organized charity fairs, and volunteered their services began to make careers for themselves in the helping professions. There arose new media and new genres for mobilizing personal giving, from telethons and marathons to megamedia events such as "Hands Across America" and "Live Aid." Not to be underestimated are the changes in sensibility—from the moral sublime to professional pride—that brought about the demise of the great charity fair, as we know it from the nineteenth century, and the concomitant changes in American Jewish public culture and the role of women in producing it.

On a Line of Hart Crane's

"And obscure as that heaven of the Jews"

In the rabbi's parable a lame one climbs
Onto a blind one's shoulders and together
They pluck the fruit of the garden of the Lord.

O body the blind one, O soul the lame one.
Soul that is never purely the soul, thank God.
The body purely the body only in Death.

Barney Cohen, Puritan mullah in the sixth grade,
Scowled at me O Little Town when I sang
The carols, and Robert you won't go to Heaven.

O Barney, where did you get that idea?
When we were in our twenties I heard he died,
In a strange accident involving LSD.

Body that trembled on the shoulders of the soul,
How still we see thee lie. Above thy deep
And dreamless sleep the silent stars go by.

Or do I misremember, and was it Barney
Whose body was attracted by the carol?
Was mine the priggish soul that scolded him

Away from those *traif* hymns, thy dark streets shineth?
Purity of Sheohl, dappled impurity of life—
The ancient Jewish community included

Many who were not Jewish, the *ger toshav*.
In the pre-Christian Empire, Greek-speaking gentiles
Joined the synagogue body without conversion.

Is anyone ever entirely in the synagogue,
O Little Town? Or ever entirely outside it?
When the great Maimonides temporizes upon

The nature of the Jewish resurrection,
A whirring of subtle wings, a storied shadow.
And if we lack a heaven shall we construct one—

With bannisters of pearl, six-pointed stars
And cartoon harps? Or Milton's eternal shampoo?
With nectar pure his oozy locks he laves.

A generation named their children Milton
And Sidney and Herbert: names of a past and a future:
An old world on the shoulders of the new,

A new world on the shoulders of the old.
The convert Hopkins thanks God for dappled things.
Barney I wish I could take you onto my shoulders

Into the Vilna Shul on Adams Street
Where an immigrant master carver from Ukraine,
Sam Katz, who specialized in merry-go-rounds

Has made a Holy Ark adorned with light bulbs
And shapes like manes and tails. How silently
The wondrous gifts are given, the freckled-forth,

Obscure inventions. Blessed is the dotted
And spotted tabernacle. O lame and blind—
O mottled town, that harbors our hopes and fears.

—*Robert Pinsky*

ARIEL SEGAL

Jews of the Amazon

Voices from the Earthly Paradise

THIS IS a story of Jewish survival or, rather, a story about the survival of a strong sense of Jewishness among people who might easily have lost their Jewish heritage in the Peruvian Amazon, the place where they had lived isolated from the neighboring Jewish communities of Brazil and Peru for more than a century.

In 1995 I visited the city of Iquitos, in the Peruvian rain forest, to research the history and identity of a community of descendants of Jews who came to this South American region from Morocco and Europe during the rubber boom of the late nineteenth and early twentieth centuries. The members of the self-proclaimed Jewish Society of Iquitos whom I met—more than one hundred people—were the offspring of mixed marriages between Jewish immigrants (overwhelmingly men) and native Amazonians. After almost a century they had organized themselves as a religious community; they still felt Jewish despite the enormous influence of Christian and other beliefs that had become part of their syncretic identity in the isolation of the rain forest.

This community is the subject of my book, *Jews of the Amazon: Self-Exile in Earthly Paradise.*[1] I call them "Jewish mestizos," since the word *mestizo,* in Spanish, refers to people who biologically descend from couples of different ethnic or racial groups. Culturally, it refers to people who inherit a syncretic identity composed of diverse legacies.

I could have limited myself to writing the history of the Jews who came to the Peruvian Amazon in the 1880s, crossing the Atlantic when the rubber boom transformed the region into a wealthy place, dreaming of becoming rich quickly, and seizing the opportunity to escape harsh conditions, especially in Morocco. Initially, these adventurous foreign fortune seekers had no intention of remaining in the jungle, but an unavoidable fact of life—death—forced them to build a Jewish cemetery in the prosperous city of Iquitos. This later became

Facade of Cohen and Company, a Jewish business in Iquitos, Peru. Photograph by Robin Cembalest.

the focal point of their community. Nevertheless, these immigrants did not build a synagogue, being content with conducting some holy day services in private homes.

I could have written only about these immigrants and avoided delving into other topics that would make my work more complex. But being in Iquitos and getting to know the children, grandchildren, and great-grandchildren of these immigrants, I could not avoid focusing my research on their identity, on the fascinating community that felt proudly Jewish as it celebrated the main Jewish holy days and rituals. As I remarked in my book, the Jews of Iquitos "dwell within a collage of religions and legacies that seem to contradict one another to the foreign eye, but they experience their legacies as a perfectly harmonious system of life. . . . They know how to maneuver among contradictions."[2] Can Jews from mainstream communities maneuver among their contradictions as fluidly as these Jewish mestizos do? Do I myself manage to experience the complexity of my Jewishness as harmoniously? Do most contemporary Jews?

My book about the Jews of the Amazon is a story about identity: theirs, mine, and that of many Jews throughout the world. In my literary works in Spanish I deal constantly with my own identity as a Venezuelan, a Jew, a person who studied and became a scholar in the United States, a lover of Israel (I am an Israeli citizen), and a man who finds significant the complex and contradictory essence of being Jewish in multicultural societies. Perhaps the simple but nuanced way the Jewish mestizos of Iquitos experience their identity is what captivated me as a historian, as a writer, but also as a Jew. Of course, contradictions are part of any identity, and pinpointing the apparent inconsistencies in other people's identities is easier than deciphering inconsistencies in one's own.

I met with people who flowed over their contradictions as naturally as the Amazon River flows between its banks. The clue for understanding the Jewishness of the descendants of Jews who got lost in their lust for native Amazonian women may be deciphered by listening to their voices—voices that have been ignored for decades, even by their fellow Jews in the capital city of Peru. I was surprised to learn that most of the Jews of Lima did not know that there had been an important migration of Jews to another part of their country, or that people of the third, fourth, and fifth generations of these immigrants still lived in the rain forest. This is an indication of the longtime isolation of these Jews and their descendants.

Why are Iquitos and its surrounding cities and towns so isolated? Until the early twentieth century Iquitos was one of the three most isolated cities in the world, along with Lhasa in Tibet and Timbuktu in the Sahara Desert. It is surrounded by the Amazon River and two of its tributaries, as well as by the biggest rain forest in the world. In addition, Iquitos is separated from the main coastal cities of Peru by 1,200 miles that include the huge Andean summits. Neither railroads nor highways pass through the city, and only after the first flights from Lima to the Peruvian Amazon in the late 1920s was the region gradually incorporated into the socioeconomic and political life of the country.

This explains why the Jewish immigrants in the main coastal cities of Peru "discovered" the presence of Jews—chiefly the first generation of Jewish mestizos—in the Amazon only in the 1930s and 1940s. By the time contacts between the two communities had become more frequent, the Jews of Lima saw the Iquitos Jews as exotic, more similar to Peruvian natives from the jungle than to Jews from the major Jewish communities of the world. Distance, topography, and even racial prejudice led the mainstream Jewish communities of Lima and the Brazilian Amazon to ignore the Amazon Jews' desire to connect with them. Nevertheless, most of the Jewish mestizos continued to try to preserve elements of their Jewishness. In the 1990s, following the example of their Jewish ancestors, they founded the Jewish Society of Iquitos in order to celebrate the main Jewish holy days, and they began to restore the Jewish cemetery established by their ancestors in 1895.

My visit to Iquitos changed my life, not only because I uncovered important material for my doctoral dissertation and later a book, but also because it taught me things about myself as a Jew and as a human being. I learned that in

The Jewish cemetery in Iquitos. Photograph by Robin Cembalest.

spite of their complex identity these Jews are able, by means of a secret code, to preserve their Jewish roots and experience their Jewishness almost without conflict.

Some may consider this claim the sentimental response of a writer, a misleading perception about a community of people who define themselves as Jews, even when most of them cannot distinguish Christian beliefs and rituals from Jewish ones. But could I deny that I was among Jews when I was watching them celebrate Kabbalat Shabbat services and Jewish holy days and prepare themselves to visit or live in the state of Israel? Can we ignore that they are descendants of Jewish ancestors and today form the only organized Jewish community in Peru, aside from the one in Lima, that still buries its members in a Jewish cemetery? This fascinating community can contribute deeply to the eternal discussion of what it is to be a Jew.

The members of this community—approximately 150 are officially registered in the Jewish Society of Iquitos—deserve to be heard so that we can grasp the wonderful aspects of Judaism they still reveal. Some of the things they think and feel might seem strange to us but obviously matter deeply to them.

Regarding *kashrut*, dietary laws, all the Iquitos Jews have some idea what Jews are allowed or forbidden to eat, but, as with most secular Jews, they do not all follow the laws. They know that pork is forbidden, and a few know that they are not supposed to eat fish without scales. They have a number of explanations for the injunction against pork. Three examples will suffice. Saul Benamú Gonzales, a third-generation descendant of a Jewish immigrant—who would be considered a Gentile from an Orthodox perspective, but who is a potential Israeli citizen with full rights according to the Israeli Law of Return—told me, "The reason why we should not eat pork is because Jews were very wise in the past, in ancient times. They knew that this is not hygienic food and therefore they were prohibited from eating it. Regarding fish without scales, you know that I have been a sailor for many years, so I learned that these kinds of fish are the ones that you find in the bottom of the rivers and they need to be cleaned. They eat what contaminates the waters, and this also was known by our wise ancestors. So I guess that this is the reason why they made a law about this."[3] Many Jews around the world might use a similar scientific argument for kashrut. On the other hand, a twenty-year-old Amazon Jew told me that she thinks that Jews are not allowed to eat pork because "it was the food Jesus ate during the Last Supper; therefore we cannot eat it."[4]

Mr. Bento, the ninety-two-year-old son of a Portuguese Jewish father, had yet another reason. After I finished interviewing him and stopped the tape recorder, he suddenly said that he had something very important to tell me (many times people told their most intimate stories after we had stopped recording—the machine intimidated them). Bento said, "Ariel, before you leave, do you know why Jews do not eat pork?" I said no, I didn't.

Mr. Bento used a specific word for "pork," *marrano.* This was the term used by Christians to refer to Jews who were forced to convert to Christianity during the time of the Inquisition in the Iberian Peninsula. In Spanish it means "pig," and it became popular to call the New Christians or converted Jews by this derogatory name to remind them that they were born not Christians, but "pigs," "dirty Jews." Today, scholars use the word *Marrano* for converted Jews without any negative connotation intended, and many non–Spanish speakers do not know that it is one of the words used to refer to pigs or pork.

So after asking me whether I knew why Jews did not eat marrano (pork), Mr. Bento explained: "A few days ago I was reading the *Reader's Digest* [in Spanish], and there was an article about the Marranos. I read that a few years ago [he did not say "a few centuries ago"] the Inquisition in Spain and Portugal converted Jews into Marranos, and you cannot eat your brother!"[5] I refrained from laughing, because I wanted to be respectful of the person in front of me, but I found his interpretation of Jews transformed literally into pigs amusing. Later, I realized that what he had told me is based on Amazonian cosmology. According to some Indian tribes everything in nature—trees, animals, clouds—was once a human being and a spirit of the jungle. Since birds, dolphins, and other animals were once human beings, why could Jews not be transformed into pigs in Spain and Portugal? In the Amazon this story makes perfect sense.

These legends and stories come naturally to people who breathe the Amazon air and experience life in a city in the middle of the jungle. When you navigate the rivers, behold the magnificence of the rain forest, and listen to the whisper of the water and the rustle of the wind over the leaves, you feel the power of the vast world of nature and start to believe that anything is possible. Then you can understand that in that place, in the Amazon, the people are telling you truths, they are knowledgeable about the rules of their world, and it is the visitors and scholars who come to the region with their big egos and ethnocentric views who must learn to be humble about their perceptions and cosmologies. Some Jews believe in dybbuks or *ain ha raa* (bad luck), while others consider such things superstitions, so why see the transformation of spirits of the jungle as a primitive notion? Some ideas that are accepted as truth in New York and other places in the world would be perceived as ridiculous by Amazonians. Through my understanding of these people my role as a historian began to undergo a change, and I realized that in their city I was the ignorant one. I was learning from people who understood and interpreted their reality in a coherent way.

It is with this perspective that we can understand how Christian, Jewish, and Amazonian traditions are able to intertwine without contradiction in Iquitos. Consider, for example, the way the Amazon Jews perceive the figure of Jesus. Most of them wonder why other Jews do not believe that Jesus was the messiah. Many of them also attend church on Sundays and are exposed to the message of the Gospels. They feel confused when the leaders of their community demand that they put aside their worship of Jesus during Shabbat services.

Here are some of the things they told me about Jesus: "Those who believe in Jesus Christ are not 100 percent Jewish." "I personally believe that the messiah has already come. I don't know whether Israel, the Jewish people, are blind. I am a Jewish believer in Christ." "Can the Jews convert believers of Jesus? It is said that Jews are more Jewish when they believe in Jesus. Thereby, one is a total Jew. Someone told me [that]; I do not know so much." "I never have understood why Jews do not believe in Christ and I haven't dared to ask."

In the meetings of the Jewish Society of Iquitos, especially during Shabbat services, the leaders of the community – Víctor Edery, the spiritual guide, and Jaime Vásquez, the general secretary – constantly explain why Jews do not believe in Jesus as God's incarnation. They repeat the explanation over and over, fighting against the tendency of many members, who barely understand the issue, to attend Christian churches as well as synagogue. This is the reason why many Jewish descendants speak about their Judaism in terms of percentages, saying, for example, "I believe in Jesus, therefore I am 25 percent Jewish." Those who do not believe in Christ can be described as "100 percent Jewish."

The stories that reveal the intertwining of Amazonian, Christian, and Jewish beliefs and traditions in Iquitos are countless. I shall mention only a few. One day, in 1992, the community gathered to bury a Mr. Toledano in the Jewish cemetery, as he had stipulated in his will. However, the family held a Christian funeral at his house first, and then all the people went to the Jewish cemetery for the burial. A priest officiated, but because Toledano had belonged to the Jewish Society, Edery and Vásquez recited the Kaddish in Spanish (they have a few *siddurim*, or prayerbooks). When they finished saying the Kaddish, they said amen, and the mourners all crossed themselves.

Other voices: there is a woman who prepares potions to help people in trouble. She makes chains with regional symbols (the equivalent of the Jewish open hand, the *Hamtza*) intended to ward against the "evil eye." She told me that for descendants of Jews, the symbol she uses is the Star of David because it protects them from the bad spirits of the jungle better than other amulets do. Yet along with this syncretism, there is pride in this community about being Jewish. In the diary I kept in the Amazon I made this entry about the founder of the Jewish Society of Iquitos:

> Don Víctor Edery Morales, the seventy-five-year-old son of a Moroccan immigrant, is the leader of the Sociedad de Beneficiencia de Iquitos and its spiritual guide. "He is the flame that refuses to be extinguished," as one *Iquiteño* defined it; the burning bush witnessed by Moses, as a Jewish poet might say.
>
> Don Víctor's bedroom serves as an idiosyncratic demonstration of the blending of Jewish historical consciousness with Amazonian cultural paradigms. Tottering, tin-plated shelves are filled with books about Christianity, Islam, Buddhism, and Daoism ("a Jew must learn about other religions," he insists), metaphysics, and, of course, *Kabbalah*, Jewish history, and Jewish rituals. Among the books one can see a poster of the ancient walled city of Jerusalem, a postcard of the former Israeli Prime Minister David Ben-Gurion, a pile of pictures of his family in Israel, Montreal, Miami, and Iquitos, and old photographs of his father. Hanging on the wall is a silver *Shalom* next to a menorah, which barely conceals a poster of a frankly voluptuous woman. All over the wall a gallery of sex symbols keeps company with the woman who "poses for the menorah." On a wooden table that functions as his desk, Don Víctor keeps plastic bags containing

> the Hebrew Bible, prayer shawls, a colorful ornamented Moroccan *kippah* (skull cap), and Hebrew prayerbooks covered with pictures of beautiful women ("You know, I use these to cover the books and protect them from the dust"). I make a joke about the pictures, and he explains with a smile that shows his broken teeth: "These posters and pictures remind me of when I was a *chibolito* [very young person] and I had women like these."
>
> The sacred and the profane mix together in this bedroom, which epitomizes the community members' seamless way of balancing what, to a foreign eye, seems contradictory, or, rather, unsuitable. Don Víctor spends a couple of hours proudly showing me each possession: books and pictures, gifts from Israel, and objects from the Amazon. He explains everything as if he were lecturing an audience: "This is a picture of David Ben-Gurion, the hero of Israel's independence, and these are pictures of my sons Yared and Víctor when they fought in the Yom Kippur War in Israel. . . . This is my mother, my daughter in Israel, and that? . . . that is a woman that I liked, she lives nearby!" Why does he not spend his last years in Israel? Don Víctor Edery meditates and at a leisurely pace answers: "I have a mission in Iquitos. Besides, I want to be buried next to my father in the Jewish cemetery."[6]

Edery passed away in 2003.

For Kabbalat Shabbat services, the community used to gather in a room next to Edery's bar every Friday at six o'clock in the evening to pray, reading their Spanish-language prayerbooks. They wanted me to lead the prayer, but I refused to do so the first two months I was there because I wanted to watch the way they did it. Thus, in my role as historian I suppressed my own instinct to teach them to say some of the prayers in Hebrew.

They had only a few prayerbooks, which they passed around so each member of the congregation could read a part of the service. They managed to conduct the service in the best way they could. The only part they read in Hebrew —using phonetics—was the Kiddush, or blessing of the wine and bread. But they insisted: "Ariel, you have to teach us how to pray in Hebrew a little bit." So one day I went to the home of Jaime Vásquez, who led the services on Fridays, and recorded some Hebrew prayers and songs for the Shabbat service for him so he could sing them himself. Vásquez was an opera singer and a professor of music and history. He persuaded me to teach him some Hebrew songs and prayers by telling me that even though many Jews had visited Iquitos and had come to the Shabbat services, none of them had bothered to teach the community anything.

That day at his home Vásquez played the violin and surprised me with two melodies. One was a Sephardic lullaby that I identified as a Ladino song; he claimed that his mother used to sing it to him when he was a child. The second was "Afn Pripetshik," a Yiddish song. I said to him: "One second! Your mother couldn't have sung that. She was Sephardic, she was descended from Sephardic Jews, so how could she have learned that song?" He said: "Okay Ariel, I will tell you the truth. I went to see *Schindler's List*, and I learned it." I happened to have the lyrics of that song in phonetics in my wallet, so we recorded it together with some Shabbat prayers, such as Lecha Dodi and Yedid Nefesh. The next week, Vásquez delighted us with his great voice during the Shabbat service, singing the prayers and "Afn Pripetshik."

Stories like these made me write in my diary:

> Tonight I do not want to see them through a scientific lens or a scholar's microscope. I am enjoying their universe, their spiritual wealth despite their apparent poverty. There is more "purity" in these old houses, with their dirty water and mosquitoes, than in the tidy temples and the rooms of the hollow homes of many Jews in big cities.
>
> I feel tired. It has been a long, long day. The more I become involved with them, the less scientific I want to be. I promised myself that I wouldn't participate in the Shabbat service, but Don Víctor Edery blessed me as "their special guest," so I agreed to sing them a couple of Shabbat songs. They listened to me as if I were Pavarotti . . . half Pavarotti, to avoid exaggerations! This time I did not fulfill my pledge to remain distant as an observer.[7]

My encounter with the Jewish mestizos developed into the story of a researcher's relationship with his living sources of information. The history of their ancestors, the original Jews who lived in Iquitos, is intriguing, but I found that the real subjects of my investigation were the people telling me the stories of their grandparents and their Jewish-Christian-Amazonian identity.

This is a community of descendants of Jews with a dual faith that they inherited from their ancestors: "I am Catholic, but I take the best from every place," one said. "All religions are good, because they give you a life with laws and a belief in God. After death, I can go to a good place. I am not completely Jewish, because I do not carry out all the customs," said another. "We are Catholics, but we always ask for the Jewish God," say others, and "We Jews belong to a chosen race, but unfortunately I am not 100 percent Jewish."

I propose a new definition of Marranism that goes beyond the compulsory conversion of Jews to another religion – specifically, to Christianity. My Marranism is the result of the natural assimilation within a group of an indigenous religious system with that group's Jewish heritage. This concept of Marranism, as a phenomenon rather than as a specific historical episode of the Middle Ages, applies to such communities as the Dohme Jews of Turkey, who were forced to convert to Islam in Salonika (today Thessaloníki, Greece) in 1666, yet retained some of their Jewish observances until the mid-twentieth century in Bulgaria, the Balkan states, and other places. It also includes the Bene Israel of Bombay, a racially mixed group that has blended Hindu customs and behaviors with Jewish rituals, sharing similar Marranic patterns. Most of the Bene Israel Jews now live in Israel.

The Marranic identity can be grasped better in the case of the descendants of the converted Jews of the isolated little town of Belmonte, Portugal, who were forced to become Christians during the Inquisition. This is the only community of Marrano descendants that continues to preserve Jewish traditions up to the present. In Belmonte, Marranos still close their windows and doors when they say Shabbat prayers or celebrate Passover in their homes. They believe that closing their doors and windows is part of tradition, and no longer remember why they do it. Outside their homes they are Christians; they go to church and celebrate Christmas and even Easter, but they feel different from the rest of the people in the town, and they know that they have Jewish blood.

This dual identity is very similar to that of the Jewish mestizos in the Amazon. Theirs, too, is a Marranism that derives from isolation, and the preservation of their Judaism is the main source of their identity. This unusual definition of Marranism might seem untenable to some scholars, but beyond the shared identity implied by the term, I see clear similarities between the Jews of Iquitos and those of similar communities, such as the Marranos of Belmonte.

It is important to take into account that even though the first Marranos retained their traditional Jewish cosmology, their descendants began to mingle elements of their Jewish and Christian heritages. Most of them practiced combined aspects of Judaism and Christianity, until a few of them—especially the crypto-Jews—returned to Judaism in places like Amsterdam and Turkey. Most of the Marranos have assimilated to Christianity. In this sense, the cosmology of the Jewish mestizos is probably closer to that of the children and grandchildren of the first converted Jews or of the ancestors of Belmonte's community of Marranos.

The isolation of the Belmonte Marranos may have helped them retain their Jewish practices. The Inquisition did not reach their part of Portugal, so these Marranos were able to continue practicing Jewish rituals in secrecy. In Iquitos, the question is: How did the descendants of the Jewish immigrants manage to preserve their Jewishness, rather than assimilate to the rest of society?

There are "rational" explanations—I use the word *rational* carefully because

I do not believe in a clear dichotomy between the rational and nonrational aspects of our lives and identities. The Jewish cemetery, for example, is a physical space that helps the Jewish mestizos feel a connection with their ancestors. Many of them described their deep feelings about the Jewish cemetery: "This is our Wailing Wall"; "I go there to listen to the voices of my grandparents."

Iquitos is a very homogeneous city, whose inhabitants are almost all poor, though they are less conscious of their poverty than poor people in many cities because the few rich inhabitants of Iquitos behave and dress the same way the poor do. There is a sense there of equality and tolerance—that is why I play with the concept of earthly paradise in my book—and this environment of openness allows the Amazonian Jews to feel free to practice their traditions without fear. Just as the Spanish Inquisition did not reach northern Portugal, so its functionaries never got to the Amazon. In this homogeneous place, what makes people feel different from one another is their past, their ancestors. The Iquiteños like to trace where they came from: France, Germany, Spain, or what some call their Jewish origins. To be a descendant of European immigrants, including Jews, gives many Iquiteños a sense of aristocracy. This is an important element of the pride the Jewish mestizos feel for their Jewish heritage. In addition, the Jewish immigrants were very successful in the commercial life of the city, and many had political and public roles there.

After the 1960s, when the Amazon was declared a tax-free region for a few years, the Iquitos Jews had a few contacts with the Jews of Lima. Ashkenazic and Sephardic Jews from Lima were excited to meet the Jewish mestizos from the Peruvian Amazon. The Orthodox rabbis, however, have not wanted to help the mestizos return to their roots. Only the Conservative rabbi Guillermo Bronstein has been willing to go to Iquitos to help the mestizos study Judaism and better organize their community. Together with other rabbis he has converted dozens of them, thereby enabling them to make *aliyah* under the Israeli Law of Return. Since 1997, when I moved to Israel, more than eighty people from the Iquitos community have established themselves there, and some of these are preparing themselves for conversion to Orthodox Judaism.

Although I can enumerate a few other reasons why the Jewish mestizos still feel Jewish, there are less isolated places in the world where Jews did assimilate. Even in Peru, Jewish communities in provinces closer to Lima have vanished. Therefore, I am not convinced that all the data I gathered and analyzed to explain the survival of this community are enough to show why it did not have the same fate as the others. I use, as a literary tool, the term "Jewish obsession syndrome" to explain what I cannot understand, this community's amazing survival.

The few Liman Jews who have visited Iquitos see the Jews there as exotics and do not take them seriously as Jews. I stress the fact that this community never had a synagogue, a religious school, or a rabbi; they did not even have a teacher to help them keep the traditions they preserve. Some of my friends in Lima and elsewhere see my enthusiasm for this community as an "anthropological hobby."

But two excerpts from my diary may help explain why the Jewish mestizos can be considered a Marranic community, even an example of Jewish survival:

> Some images and voices from the past few weeks are hovering in my mind: a Star of David and a cross together on a chain and on a gravestone. An old woman tells me the history of her Jewish ancestry; she tells me how proud she is of belonging to the chosen people, and then she asks me why Jews don't accept Christ as God, as if that is an unquestionable fact.
>
> More images: one of the leaders of the Jewish community, whose house has become the prayer site for every Shabbat, is raising a pig in his backyard for a future banquet. The girl who learned in a week to recite the *Shalom Aleichem* prayer in Hebrew because she is preparing for a one-way trip to Israel lights candles and dances for a saint so that her Zionist dream will materialize. Someone who never cared about his Jewish origin asks to be buried in the Jewish cemetery. The president of a Jewish institution suggests a Christmas party, while another member of the institution expresses his excitement about organizing a "fiesta" for Yom Kippur (until he is told that there are "fiestas," holidays, on which Jews do not drink and dance). . . .
>
> It is June 1995. I meet Ronald Reategui Levy [the current president of the community] in a café. He tells me about his wife; his two sons, Uri and Netaniel; his job; his dream of immigrating to the Holy Land; his problems finding somebody to help him realize that dream; his readiness to leave if he can work in the oil fields or in agriculture ("You have to see my garden; I make hybrid plants"); his house ("You have to see it, especially my front door"). Finally, he tells me how he has improved his Hebrew. Trained to be skeptical, I begin to ask him questions in Hebrew, and he answers me in good Hebrew. "How did you learn?" I ask him. He replies, "I learned the Hebrew letters thanks toYared Edery and a few classes I attended in Lima (I lived there a few months); the vocabulary I picked up with my Hebrew Bible and a dictionary. I also spent two months in an *ulpan* [Hebrew class] in Lima," he tells me. "You know, the nights in the oil fields are long and the workers gather to drink and talk. I spent my hours in my room reading the Bible with my dictionary. I have been doing that for more than seven years."
>
> It takes me a while to realize that he is not exaggerating, that he really speaks Hebrew, that he really read the *Kuzari* of [the medieval Jewish poet

and philosopher] Yehuda HaLevi, a book that many secular Jews have never even heard of. So I decided to go to his house. What does he want to show me? Yes, his garden; yes, his fish pond; yes, his wife and children, and the front door. What is so special about it? When you visit a humble, tin-roofed house on the perimeter of Iquitos, a grim zone of small, scattered houses where everybody is a farmer, and you see a wooden door with a huge carved Star of David, a menorah, and the Hebrew words *Beth Levi* (House of Levi), there are reasons to feel a tug at the heart. I am really in front of a Jewish house in the middle of the Amazon jungle. I am before something that makes me feel very small. I thought I was coming from a big universe to a little town, but I have just traveled from the little town of my big aspirations to the huge universe where the star on that door is located.[8]

A doorway with a mezuzah in Iquitos. Photograph by Robin Cembalest.

The journalist Michael Freund visited Iquitos with me and Rabbi Eliyahu Birnbaum, a judge who sits on Israel's rabbinical conversion courts. He wrote about Ronald Reategui Levy and the efforts of the community to learn, to convert to Judaism, and to establish themselves in the state of Israel. Levy told Freund that about two hundred members of the community had already immigrated to Israel and a hundred more were preparing to go. "'It is not easy to be a Jew here, because of the many difficulties,'" Levy told Freund. "'People study and convert here, and then make *aliya.* Once in Israel, they complete what they have started here.'" The Jewish Agency representative in Peru elaborated: "'They feel very strongly about Judaism, and they want to live in the land of their ancestors. They know that for them and for their children it will be a better future.'"[9]

The story of the Iquitos community continues, with sequels in the Peruvian Amazon, in Lima, and now in the state of Israel. It is a story that can be studied on a historical, an anthropological, or a sociological basis. My contribution has gone beyond academia and is now in the hands of rabbis, Israeli functionaries, and politicians. But the story of the Iquitos Jews demonstrates their deep attachment to Judaism, their Jewish obsession syndrome. This is what the medieval philosopher Ibn Verga warned the king of Spain about, in a letter responding to the king's decision to expel the Jews from their homes in 1492: "Know, sir, that Judaism, in spite of all its challenges, is an incurable disease."

Immature Song

I have heard that adolescence is a recent invention,
A by-product of progress, one of Capitalism's

Suspended transitions between one state and another,
Like refugee camps, internment camps, like the Fields

Of Concentration in a campus catalogue. Summer
Camps for teenagers. When I was quite young

My miscomprehension was that "Concentration Camp"
Meant where the scorned were admonished to concentrate,

Humiliated: forbidden to let the mind wander away.
"Concentration" seemed just the kind of punitive euphemism

The adult world used to coerce, like the word "Citizenship"
On the report cards, graded along with disciplines like History

English, Mathematics. Citizenship was a field or
Discipline in which for certain years I was awarded every

Marking period a "D" meaning Poor. Possibly my first political
Emotion was wishing they would call it Conduct, or Deportment.

The indefinitely suspended transition of the refugee camps
Must be a poor kind of refuge, with its subjection to capricious

Kindness and requirements and brutality, the unchampioned
Refugees kept between childhood and adulthood, with neither.

In the Holy Land for example, or in Mother Africa.
At that same time of my life when I heard the abbreviation

"DP" for Displaced Person I somehow mixed it up with
"DT's" for Delirium Tremens, both a kind of stumbling called

By a childish nickname. And you my poem, you are like
An adolescent: confused, awkward, self-preoccupied, vaguely

Rebellious in a way that lacks practical focus, moving without
Discipline from thing to thing. Do you disrespect Authority merely

Because it speaks so badly, because it deploys the lethal bromides
With a clumsy conviction that offends your delicate senses? —but if

Called on to argue such matters as the refugees you mumble and
Stammer, poor citizen, you get sullen, you sigh and you look away.

—*Robert Pinsky*

DONALD KUSPIT

Meyer Schapiro's Jewish Unconscious

Meyer Schapiro, Self-Portrait, Brussels, *1923. Conté crayon on paper, 11 × 8½ in. (27.9 × 21.6 cm). The Jewish Museum, Gift of the artist, 1987–86.*

In 1994, Margaret Olin, reviewing the fourth volume of Meyer Schapiro's *Selected Papers,* observed that Schapiro "only seldom addressed [his] Jewish heritage."[1] Surely, she suggests, it must have influenced his practice of art history and criticism. But she is at a loss to say how. Olin notes that Schapiro's neglect of the issue is all the more conspicuous in view of the fact that his contemporaries, the Jewish American art critics Clement Greenberg and Harold Rosenberg, openly viewed modern art from a Jewish perspective. Although it was one among several heuristic gambits, they often emphasized it as the most revelatory—the perspective that could disclose what is most at stake or immanent in modern art.

Thus, Rosenberg argued that anxiety about identity is "the most serious theme"—indeed, the ultimate "metaphysical theme"—in both Jewish life and modern art.[2] Such anxiety was at its height after World War II, which is why many Jews became artists then. Art allowed them to work through their ambivalence about being Jews. They experienced Jewish identity as increasingly problematic in the modern world, yet inescapable—even in the modern world. But it is modern to be alienated from one's received identity, which made the modern Jewish artist exemplary.

Greenberg declared that "Kafka's Jewish self . . . tests the limits of art. . . . When did a Jew ever come to terms with art without falsifying himself somehow? Does not art always make one forget what is literally happening to oneself as a certain person in a certain world? And might not the investigation of what is literally happening to oneself remain the most human, therefore, the most serious . . . of all possible activities?"[3]

Could Franz Kafka reconcile the Jew and the artist in himself? Did he use his art to understand his situation as a Jew in a Christian world? If Jews turn to art to strengthen their sense of self—to survive emotionally in a world in which they are always suspect—aren't they turning away from God? Doesn't art help one remember—indeed, embody—what emotionally happens to one in the world, and isn't that more essential than what literally happens to one?

Modern art in particular raises such questions for Greenberg, for it tends to be alienated from the world it represents. And the modern Jewish artist—most noteworthily, Kafka—has a certain ironical advantage or head start, for he or she can graft the alienation inescapable in modern life onto the alienation built into Jewish existence, the alienation that is the Jew's birthright. Thus, contrary to all expectations, the Jew is in a position, by reason of his or her emotional if not religious heritage, to become the exemplary modern artist, which is what Kafka was for Greenberg. While "the Jewish truth, or the truth of [Kafka's] Jewishness . . . accounts for some of the frustrations of his art," it also reminds us that "one of the functions of art [is] to keep contradictions in suspension, unresolved."[4] Thus, the artist is entitled to "inconsistency," however much "the triumph of art lies—as always—in [the] reconciliation" of "contradictory impulses."[5] Kafka's stories are a major test of art, for in them the impulse to make art is in conflict with the Jewish awareness of menace, even as they ingeniously use art to bring the reader to full, excruciating consciousness of it, and to transpose it to the modern world. Kafka's triumph is to make its menace unmistakable—traumatic and overwhelming.

The question as to whether Jewish identity and artistic identity can be reconciled—whether the apparent contradiction between them can be overcome—seems very far from Schapiro's thinking about modern art, and art in general. And yet, as I hope to show, it is as important for Schapiro as it is for Greenberg and Rosenberg, but much more subliminally. Like them, Schapiro was an early, forceful advocate of abstract expressionism. And like them, he thought that selfhood or identity was the central issue of modern art, as his studies of Cézanne and van Gogh indicate. But this rarely involved Jewish identity, at least overtly, as it tended to in the thinking of Greenberg and Rosenberg.

Only in Schapiro's essay on Marc Chagall's illustrations for the Bible does he explicitly deal with an artist's Jewishness, which he feels had a remarkably positive effect on the artist's work. It was because of his Jewishness that Chagall "surmounted . . . the limits of his own and perhaps all modern art," Schapiro writes. Jewishness kept him in touch with "the full range of his emotions and thoughts," unlike other modern painters, whose "enthusiasm for new and revolutionary possibilities of form and . . . desire for an autonomous personal realm" led them "to exclude large regions of experience from their work." Jewishness gave Chagall's art a broad humanity not always in evidence in modern art. Schapiro's essay is the only place I know of where he criticizes modern art; he usually praises the modern artist's preference for "the spontaneous, the immediately felt," indicating his "remarkable inner freedom." Thus, while Chagall "owes much to the happy conjunction of his Jewish culture – to which painting was alien – and modern art – to which the Bible has been a closed book," he is a "rare," virtually unique phenomenon.[6] In more ways than one: he is the only consciously Jewish artist, modern or otherwise, whom Schapiro deals with, apart from the anonymous artist who created the "bird's head" Haggadah in the fourteenth century.

The absence of sustained, explicit engagement with the question of Jewish identity in Schapiro's oeuvre is all the more surprising in view of the fact that he never denied his Jewishness, unlike the great connoisseur Bernard Berenson, who actively repudiated his Jewishness by converting to Christianity. Berenson initially became an Episcopalian – the thing to be at Harvard and in the world of Boston Brahmins that Berenson moved in – and then converted again, becoming a Catholic, supposedly out of love for the woman who became his wife but also because it was the thing to be in Italy, where Berenson settled. Sounding like an anti-Semite, Berenson in fact once wrote that "the puzzling character of the Jews . . . and their interests are too vitally opposed to *ours* to permit the existence of that intelligent sympathy between *us* and them" (emphasis mine).

I am quoting from "Mr. Berenson's Values," Schapiro's notorious 1961 essay on Berenson.[7] Schapiro's title clearly suggests his determination to separate his values from those of Berenson. Berenson's disavowal of his Jewishness – his identification of himself as a Christian – is completely alien and repugnant to Schapiro. Olin focuses on the essay, correctly regarding it as essential for understanding Schapiro. It reveals not only, as she writes, "the complexities of the experience of Jewish art historians and critics" but the Jewish thread in Schapiro's labyrinthine writing about art.[8] To use Henry James's phrase, the essay strongly suggests that a Jewish figure can be deciphered in the carpet of Schapiro's consciousness of art, if one cares to look carefully. Jewish identity is the irrepressible issue of Schapiro's discussion of Berenson, leading one to suspect that it must be inherent in his outlook, if usually unconscious. It is as though, dealing with Berenson, Schapiro could no longer repress himself, for

Berenson's denial of his Jewish heritage—a temptation for many assimilated Jews, indeed, a confirmation of their assimilation (at least in their minds)—was inseparable from his achievement. And yet, as Schapiro subtly shows, it was a peculiarly Jewish achievement: Berenson's Jewish identity gave him the strength of character and cunning to survive and flourish in alien circumstances. Schapiro's essay is a remarkable tour de force: a vigorous, if ironical affirmation of the benefits of a Jewish identity. More crucially, Berenson forced Schapiro to show his hand—to signal, decisively if only once, the important, even crucial role Jewish identity played in his view of art. Indeed, I will argue that for Schapiro the most innovative artists were Jewish in spirit—that he believed authentic innovation was possible only from a "Jewish position" in society.

Schapiro deals with Berenson's Jewish identity at great length. Yet the index to the fourth volume of Schapiro's *Selected Papers,* in which the essay is reprinted, does not mention Jewishness. In general, there are few references to Jewishness in any index in any volume of the *Selected Papers.* In the index to volume three, devoted to late antique, early Christian, and medieval art, mention is made of "Jewish art," "Jewish literature and folklore," and the (good) relations between Jews and Christians in the Carolingian Empire. But apart from that, only the first volume, on Romanesque art, discusses "Jewish beliefs." Two of the five references are to footnotes. The relative paucity of reference to things Jewish is no doubt predictable in the context of an analysis of Christian art. But, as I will argue, it is the fact that they occur in this context that gives them peculiar weight.

Berenson and Schapiro had a certain amount in common. Both were Lithuanian Jews, born almost forty years apart, Berenson in 1865 and Schapiro in 1904. Yiddish was their first language. But Schapiro never changed the surname that identified him as a Jew, while Valvrojensky became Berenson. And Berenson's birthplace was no longer Butremanz but Vilna, which is the way it is still listed in the *Encyclopaedia Britannica.* Thus, Berenson falsified his identity, while Schapiro remained true to his. Noting these facts, Schapiro observes that Berenson, "through his interest in old Italian art . . . was able to surmount" the "troubling" question of his Jewish identity and origin by "transposing the questions: Who am I? Where did I come from? to the challenging problem of the identity of artists, creative personalities known by their first names" and widely admired "but often mistaken for others in the labeling of works."[9] Berenson created a new identity as a connoisseur of Italian art out of an early identity as a specialist in Oriental languages. (At Harvard he studied, apparently with rabbinical diligence and fervor, Arabic, Assyrian, Hebrew, and Sanskrit.) It paralleled his change of religious (and social) identity from Jew to

Christian. These self-transformations clearly interest Schapiro as creative solutions to the problem of identity. For Schapiro, Berenson's self-creation suggests a kind of artistic resourcefulness.

In fact, for all his skepticism about Berenson, Schapiro is not without a certain admiration for him, especially because of his ability to survive in an alien, inhospitable world. Even though Berenson was a Jew from the "uncouth ghetto," Schapiro writes, he was able to force "the New England patricians [to] meet him on the higher ground of culture, in his personally created establishment in the land of the great Renaissance painters." "A frail little man, an aesthete dreaming of Pater's Marius, [Berenson] had the will and energy and intelligence to achieve authority and a social position," as well as to make a fortune. Indeed, Schapiro remarks, not without a certain respect and perhaps surprise, "through all dangers [Berenson] landed on both feet, even under Fascist anti-Semitism and with Hitler's army in Italy during the Second World War."[10] Berenson, in fact, was a role model for Schapiro until a moment of disillusionment, which he describes in his essay. Certainly their paths were different, yet Schapiro identified with Berenson as a Jew making his way in a Christian world openly prejudiced against Jews. Berenson's will to survive and even flourish, materially and intellectually, against all odds, testifies, for Schapiro, to his Jewish pride. Thus, Berenson remained a Jew on the inside, however much, on the outside, he denied that he was one.

In his Berenson essay, Schapiro makes it clear that he is deeply concerned with Jewish identity and, more crucially, its relationship to artistic creativity. But this concern is, paradoxically, not generally visible on the surface of his writing (perhaps because it is deep). Nonetheless, it is possible to infer, and demonstrate, that for Schapiro the creative, paradoxical way Jews—Jews like Berenson—survive and establish an identity in a world that barely tolerates their existence is the model for the way artists achieve their creative identity. That is, the paradox that art becomes when it is most creative exemplifies what might be called the "Jewish paradox." I will offer a reading of Schapiro to prove my point. I will even attempt to explain why Schapiro's Jewish concerns necessarily remain hidden, however profoundly his thought is informed by them.

For Schapiro, all authentically creative art—which is not every art—is subliminally Jewish, not in a doctrinaire sense but in attitude. This holds not only for modern art, which Schapiro regards as a particular triumph of creativity, but also for the remarkable sculptures of the Romanesque abbey church of Souillac. Both show the Jewish paradox in action. For Schapiro, the achievement of creative art, in whatever society it occurs—and he studied it primarily in medieval Christian society and modern capitalist society—is Jewish in a generic sense. Thus, while Schapiro doesn't use the word *Jewish*, the negative social experience out of which artists make something aesthetically positive through creative mastery is fundamentally Jewish. The Jew's social role is to represent creative survival against great odds, which is why, however much they are persecuted, Jews are never completely exterminated; they represent society's need to believe in its survival, indeed, its immortality. The Jews have been called the "eternal people" for good reason—they carry the austere banner of eternity for society. But this is also why they are regarded ambivalently—the requirements of eternity often interfere with those of the moment. Eternity is fairly demanding; it doesn't accept half-measures. The creative artist is also a survivor—that is, a person who can establish an identity and sense of self and individuality against great odds. The artist also represents a possible immortality—truly creative art is not just made for the moment. The Jewish paradox is cross-cultural and verges on being a historical paradigm for Schapiro, but the important point is that it signals a common problem artists face wherever and whenever they live, especially if they want to be original. The Jewish paradox is, then, the root paradox of art for Schapiro. He understands its history through this paradox and at least two other paradoxes that follow from and, in a sense, explicate it. Schapiro uses them to make art, at its most creative and innovative, intelligible. I emphasize that while Schapiro is thoroughly familiar with the history of art, he concentrates on works of art that show the most originality. When Schapiro analyzes these carefully, in great empirical detail, they reveal that originality is a peculiarly paradoxical achievement.

A paradox, according to the *Oxford Universal Dictionary*, is "a statement or tenet contrary to received opinion or belief." It can also be "a statement seemingly absurd or self-contradictory, though possibly well-founded or essentially true." The prefix *para-* signifies "by the side of," often implying "amiss, faulty, irregular, disordered, improper, wrong," as well as "subsidiary relation." To what? To the orthodox, which the dictionary tells us means "right in opinion," "holding correct, i.e., currently accepted, opinions, especially in theology." *Paradox*, then, has a certain resemblance to *heterodox*, which means "not in accordance with established doctrines or opinions, or those generally recognized as orthodox," "originally in religion and theology," that is, in the theory and practice of spirituality. But paradox is not just discordant; in contradicting established doctrine it establishes self-contradiction. It carries difference to the point of absurdity. More precisely, it goes against received opinion and belief, but it does not offer a different opinion and belief. Rather, it signals the absurdity of all opinion and belief. It frees us from any and every existing opinion and belief. That is, paradox offers us spiritual liberation. It releases us from our bondage to *doxa*, to use the Greek word. Instead of doctrine, it gives us a certain sense of spirit (*Geist*).

Thus, in a paradox, opposites unite to creative, spiritual effect. What looks absurd and incoherent from the aspect of ordinary logic has a spiritual logic: the logic of transcending received doctrines of any kind, leaving one with a sense that no opinion is fixed forever—indeed, that belief is beside the point of spirit. Rather than dismissing paradox as a dead-end logical puzzle, it can be experienced as a form of play and, as such, a sign of spontaneity and freedom. Schapiro is obsessed with paradoxes. Again and again, he celebrates them as characteristic of truly original art. Indeed, they are art's ultimate gift to us.

Let me bring this down to earth. The Jew is by definition heterodox within an orthodox Christian world. That is, the Jew has different received opinions and is in the minority. In a world of Christian orthodoxy, the Jew is radically Other. Jews are by definition outsiders, not only "within the bourgeoisie," as Max Horkheimer said, but because they have a "basic common experience . . . that no degree of conformism was enough to make one's position as a member of society secure," that is, a long "experience of the tenacity of social alienation." The question is how the heterodox minority can survive the domination of the orthodox majority without being submissive and without surrendering its beliefs. The answer is by becoming creative. What does it mean to be creative? It means to establish what Schapiro calls a "chiasmic, antithetic" or "discoordinate" relationship with orthodoxy.[11] How does one do this? By treating orthodox beliefs spontaneously, which affords a certain sense of freedom from them and unwittingly undermines them or forces them to change. Spontaneity is rebellion within a system of orthodoxy and conformity, only the conforming orthodox do not realize this until it is too late for them to inhibit or censor it.

Similarly, the artist is heterodox within an orthodox world of conformity, be it Christian or capitalist. The artist has to work with its received opinions but can treat them in a spontaneous, creative way, which liberates him or her from them. If the artist is a good abstract expressionist painter, he or she produces a painting that conveys a sense that there are no received opinions—a giddy sense of spontaneity and freedom, which undoubtedly looks like anarchy to the orthodox and doctrinaire. If the artist is a sculptor working on Souillac, the artist produces a self-contradictory work of art that, by reason of its interplay of sacred and profane elements, seems to undermine the official hierarchy of being. In the case of both Jew and artist, this way of responding to the dominant, deadening, doctrinaire orthodoxy is paradoxical, and the result is a vital spiritual paradox—the core of a sense of identity. For Schapiro, art is the individual's creative solution to the problem of oppressive orthodoxy that demands conformity. The individual's nonconformist, unorthodox resources of spontaneity and inner freedom can resist and replace it.

Schapiro is acutely aware that the original work of art that embodies the individual's unorthodox solution to the problem of survival and identity in an orthodox world is likely to be aggrandized by that world as an expression of a subsidiary identity. Ironically, the work becomes proof of orthodoxy's own survival power, as well as a demonstration that, after all, it is not so oppressive. Orthodox society honors unorthodox art to show its tolerance of nonconformity and insubordination, but it does so only after the fact, that is, after it has created an oppressive world that made unorthodox originality's "insurgent" convictions necessary for survival.[12]

Thus, capitalism, the dominant orthodoxy of the modern world, turns unorthodox art into a commodity. In a famous passage, Schapiro deplores the commodification of art, which exploits its essential spirituality, to use his own word. Paradoxically, it is only as a commodity that art survives—just as, paradoxically, it was only as a Christian that the Jewish Berenson survived and was able to devote himself to eternal art. Similarly, Christianity, the dominant orthodoxy of the medieval world, assimilated Romanesque art, which is only nominally Christian. As Schapiro wrote, Romanesque art was "a new sphere of artistic creation without religious content and imbued with values of spontaneity, individual fantasy, delight in color and movement, and the expression of feeling that anticipate modern art." For Schapiro, such qualities suggest that Romanesque art, like "much of the best art of our day . . . [was] strongly critical of contemporary life," that is, the dominant Christian orthodoxy.[13]

Romanesque art and modern abstract art are the poles of Schapiro's interests. They converge. In a sense, what Romanesque art began climaxes in modern abstract art, which, "more passionately than ever before, [is] the occasion of spontaneity or intense feeling. The [abstract] painting symbolizes an individual who realizes freedom and deep engagement of the self within the work."[14] Such deep engagement is a criticism of society. Intense feeling, ostensibly religious but issuing in a new aesthetic, is implicitly critical of orthodoxy. As Schapiro argues in his brilliant analysis of the socioeconomic basis of early modernist art, the spontaneity of "early Impressionism . . . had a moral aspect. . . . Its unconventional, unregulated vision . . . [is] an implicit criticism of symbolic social and domestic formalities." It was an antidote to "a sense of helpless isolation in an anonymous, indifferent mass." But within a decade "the enjoying individual becomes rare in Impressionist art," and in neoimpressionism even "the private spectacle of nature" disintegrates. What is left is "the social group" broken up into "isolated spectators, who do not communicate with each other," as in Georges Seurat's masterpiece *La Grand Jatte* (1884–86), and the representation of "mechanically repeated dances submitted to a preordained movement with little spontaneity," as in Seurat's *Study for Le Chahut* (1889) and Toulouse-Lautrec's *Moulin de la Galette* (1888). The art of Gauguin and van Gogh is a "groping to reconstitute the pervasive human sociability that capitalism had destroyed" – to avoid the fate of the listless, numbed, ironically dispassionate figures we see in Seurat and Toulouse-Lautrec. "But since the artists did not know the underlying economic and social causes of their own disorder and moral insecurity, they could envisage new stabilizing forms only as quasi-religious beliefs or as a revival of some primitive or highly ordered traditional society with organs for a collective spiritual life."[15]

In other words, the impressionists, neoimpressionists, and symbolists were faced with the Jewish paradox. They were forced to use their creativity in a life-threatening situation over which they had no control. Schapiro dissects various artistic solutions to life-threatening capitalism and, implicitly, Christianity. The solutions, which are the result of a desperate struggle for emotional survival in an objectively oppressive society, as Schapiro emphasizes, involve the same spontaneity and inner freedom. The artist has the courage of his spontaneity and projects his inner freedom onto his art. His artistic solution to his psychosocial problems is personal, but it clearly has social import, which is why society eventually enshrines it, without necessarily understanding it. Indeed, society has to ignore the reason for originality – rebellious criticism – in order to "recognize" original art. Such a recognition invariably involves a falsifying reconceptualization of the art as purely formal.

For Schapiro, the dialectic or paradox of originality or genuine creativity involves a heterodox individual who criticizes and contradicts an orthodox system of opinion and belief with his own spontaneity and inner freedom in order to survive and establish autonomy, a word Schapiro frequently uses. The irony of originality is that the individual has to identify partially with orthodoxy to defeat it – or rather, to transform it into a symbol of himself or herself. Vestiges of orthodoxy – that is, orthodox iconography, indicative of received social opinion, orthodox style, and received conceptions of creative art (as though art were simply a mimicry and reiteration of received ideas) survive within the artist's unorthodox representations, which not only reveal orthodoxy's underlying truth but also symbolize the artist's opposition to it.

Basically, what the artist wants and creates is breathing space. The work of art is an unorthodox space in which it is possible to breathe, in an emotionally stifling orthodox society. The highest accolade Greenberg could give a work of art was to say that it breathed. Schapiro says something similar – he spells out what it means to breathe, and in fact at one point uses the same language Greenberg does.[16]

The Jew needs breathing space in the Christian world, just as the artist needs breathing space in the capitalist world. Both create breathing spaces that are perversely healthy alternatives to stuffy orthodoxy. Like the Jew, then, the artist constantly monitors a threatening environment—an environment that asks artists to sacrifice creativity to some orthodoxy and, if they refuse, tries to impose it on them. Like Berenson, the artist may, on the surface, give in to survive. (It is worth noting that the conception of art as a mode of health is Nietzschean, but Nietzsche didn't realize as fully as Schapiro its ironical character and social place. It should also be noted that, unlike Greenberg, Schapiro believes, and demonstrates, that Jewishness, as an inescapable state of mind for the sensitive individual, and art, as a creative escape from it, are not only compatible but inseparable.)

Spontaneity and inner freedom show themselves through what Schapiro calls "discoordination" and chiasmic dialectic—paradox in action, as it were. Discoordination, Schapiro writes, is "a grouping or division such that corresponding sets of elements include parts, relations, or properties which negate that correspondence."[17] A chiasmic dialectic is an unresolved dialectic, that is, one in which doubleness is more evident than unity, as Schapiro might have put it. Chiasmic or negative dialectic is the root of discoordination; it results in a discoordinated or negative aesthetic.

More directly relevant to the idea of dialectical creativity is chiasmatypy, a term from genetics that designates "the supposed spiral twisting of homologous chromosomes about each other during parasynapsis, with fusion and possible crossing over at the points of contact." Put this another way: the heterodox and orthodox, which are homologous except for one gene of belief—the crucial difference—conjugate to paradoxical effect. Schapiro explicitly asserts that this dialectical process of ironic doubling is the method of individualization or individuation. Actually, he is obsessed with the structure of opposition and its dialectical resolution in paradox. He is always disclosing the paradoxical doubleness of the works of art he investigates, or of such critics as Eugène Fromentin and Denis Diderot, who are, in their different ways, role models for him because of their awareness of doubleness.

Thus, Schapiro speaks of the "calculated ambiguity" of art, Champfleury's "double attitude . . . to the events of 1848 and 1849," the "double character of the mousetrap . . . as domestic object and theological symbol" in Robert Campin's *Mérode Altarpiece*, the "double process" whereby religious authority becomes humanized and realism spiritualized in that same altarpiece—a process basic to the most creative religious art—and a "double gesture . . . not merely designed to represent a more complex interaction, but . . . an element of a style which promotes contrasts and movement," and "constitutes an expressive form as well as an expressive symbol."[18] Important images always have a "double character," particularly in Romanesque art, and particularly images of force, in which Schapiro shows a special interest. He repeatedly analyzes "counterpart elements," "counter movements," "counterpart patterns," "counterpart symmetrical gestures," and contrasts of color and direction, as when legs vigorously cross in a stark X form.[19] He loves paradoxes of meaning, as when he notes that "just as two unlike words (or syntactical forms) may have a common ancestor, so in different languages two similar words with the same meaning may be independent of each other."[20] Thus, the paradoxical import of *saltimbanque* and *banker*, which both derive from the same bank or bench of the fairs. But the former symbolizes the impoverished yet independent artist, in theory a person of free, spontaneous, deeply feeling spirit, and as such heterodox; whereas the latter names an authority on and priest of money, a pillar of the capitalist orthodoxy.

Schapiro is taken with juggling, and any kind of juggling with words and visual forms, with the way new art negates old art while "the old may persist beside the new in affirming an opposed or declining culture," and with Augustine's dialectical conception of beauty—"God is an artist who employs antitheses of good and evil to form the beauty of the universe, and . . . where beauty is a compound of opposites, including ugliness and disorder." He loves, as he says St. Bernard did, "striking contrasts, violent and astounding oppositions . . . the antithetic and inverted." He admires Piet Mondrian's "asymmetry of unequal lines." Van Gogh's paintings achieve their agonizing quality by means of "counter-goals," "competing centers," and "competing directions." Their power derives from "crossing diagonals," their "strain" or tension from "self-conflicted" forms. Cézanne's art engages us, emotionally and intellectually, because of his "practice of the other pole," his attempt to overcome the "polarity" between color and line as well as self and nature, and in general his use of "counterpart shapes" and "color contrasts." Schapiro speaks of the "stress of contrasts" in Cézanne's paintings and the "contradictions" in those of van Gogh.[21]

In *Crows over the Wheat Field* (1890) van Gogh "is caught up across the yellow fields from the chaos of the paths and the dread of approaching birds and carried to the deep blue sky, the region of the most nuanced sensibility, a pure, all-absorbing essence in which at last subject and object, part and whole, past and present, near and far, can no longer be distinguished." Romanesque art makes similar use of chiasmic form to achieve an effect of sublimely nihilistic indistinguishability and ironical totality. "Expressive dualities," "polar forms," "polar ideas," acquire their particular weight "within a prevailing system of (social) values," just as the doubleness of the Jew's existence has its weight because of its ironical place in the prevailing system of social values. Schapiro's sense of dialectic is derived from his reading of Hegel and Marx, who offered "an explanation of active historical process," and from Alois Riegl, who examined "possible latent internal conditions" of development by analyzing the "oppositions within a style" (or society) that render it "unstable and hence suggested fresh changes and solutions."[22] But it is also derived from Schapiro's sense of being a Jew and therefore in the opposition, forced into either submission or independence, or, dialectically, some creative compromise between the two, such as Berenson in his way—and Schapiro in his way—achieved.

It has been said that psychoanalysis is a Jewish science. I would rather call it the Jewish revenge, its revenge consisting in its demonstration that there is conflict behind even the most sanctimoniously orthodox, socially unctuous facade. One might say that Schapiro devoted a good part of his career to Christian art in order to demonstrate that it is highly—indeed, violently—conflicted and full of awkward compromises, that is, contradictions and bizarre syntheses of opposites, which give the lie to the Christian profession of universal reconciliation. In doing this—in going right to the center of traditional art history, namely, the study of Christian iconography and classical or classicizing style—Schapiro subverts traditional art history, in the process turning it into what might be called a Jewish science: a science of aesthetic and moral paradoxes. Art is a matter of unbalanced psychosocial forces brought into precarious, unpredictable balance, not of divinely foreordained harmony, a preconceived unity whose historical and formal exemplification in different styles is ultimately beside the point. Also, in showing that the most dynamic Christian art is implicitly modern, he shows that art history cannot help but be modern itself—that is, the study of dynamic dialectical process—rather than the reification of existing modes of art into ideal, absolute models, which is what occurs under the guise of classification.

Schapiro needs modern art to come to his aid—which in part is why he supports it and identifies with its oppositional spontaneity and inner freedom—because he is taking on the traditional art history establishment, which is heavily invested in traditional art, and thus supports Christian orthodoxy whether it wants to or not. One has only to realize that many traditional art historians think modern art was an experiment that went awry to appreciate the courage of Schapiro's conviction. And one has to realize that Schapiro wrote next to nothing about Renaissance Christian art, which is the stronghold of traditional art history, to understand how unorthodox an art historian he is. (His most "Renaissance" essay is his response to Freud's essay on Leonardo. There, with his usual irony, he goes against psychoanalytic orthodoxy with an orthodox art historical approach.)[23]

Schapiro's vision of art stands in paradoxical opposition to traditional art history not only because it unites the traditional Christian and modern capitalist art at their most critical and intense but because in doing so it contradicts two of the most basic tenets of traditional art history: namely, that the aesthetic and the moral have nothing to do with each other, and that traditional art must be understood on its own terms, without reference to modern art and modern ideas. The first assumption is equivalent to saying that spontaneous form and social content have nothing to do with each other, a view Schapiro fiercely combats in his critique of Jurgis Baltrušaitis's conception of Romanesque art and his critique of Alfred Barr's conception of the development of abstract art.[24] The second assumption amounts to asserting that there is no continuity of human issues in art history, so that the art of the past cannot live in the present, a view he attacks in his critique of Berenson's attitude toward modern art. For Schapiro, both assumptions reduce the living art of the past and present to irrelevance and inhumanity. They do this by denying the enduring human, subjective purpose of formal innovation.

Formal innovation is always motivated by the desperate wish to maintain the feeling of being emotionally alive and autonomous, as he argues in his 1960 essay "On the Humanity of Abstract Painting." Abstract art, as he writes in his 1957 essay "Recent Abstract Painting," reflects "the pathos of the reduction or fragility of the self within a culture that [is] increasingly organized through industry, economy and the state," a potentially fascist situation that "intensifies the desire of the artist to create forms that will manifest in liberty."[25] Orthodoxy carried to an extreme becomes fascist, squeezing out, even obliterating the sense of selfhood, which turns to art to rescue and preserve itself. In general, Schapiro's essays on modern art are an implicit critique of the totalitarian and authoritarian tendencies of Christian orthodoxy. This is part of their creative Jewishness. Genuinely creative art, like creative Jewishness — the Jewishness of Schapiro and, to a lesser extent, Berenson — is a mode of adaptation to an oppressive society, and as such a declaration of independence and liberty, which is why, as Schapiro says, it moves us deeply. It reminds us that even in the most impossible circumstances we can survive and even have autonomy, if only inwardly.

The two paradoxes through which Schapiro understands art history are variations of the Jewish paradox. The first paradox, that one can understand the sociomoral issues implicit in art only by understanding its aesthetic character, is encapsulated in his assertion that "aesthetic feeling . . . [can] be a starting point of radical thought"; "the aesthetic . . . [can] sublimate the imperfections of the world," and in doing so criticizes it. If aesthetics is not a spiritual transformation of "common experience," and if it does not address "the problems of mankind," then art "risks becoming empty and sterile." For Schapiro, the contradiction between aesthetic spontaneity and moral content first appeared, in its modern form, in Diderot's thought. Diderot resolved it by imagining an art of "passionate morality." While being "an ethics of altruism" and an "implicit critique of egoistic indulgence," such an art nonetheless conveyed "the general principle" that "art in modern society requires for its life the artist's spontaneity." According to Schapiro, Diderot was among the first to recognize this principle and regard spontaneity as a moral, indeed, altruistic matter. Of course, Schapiro, with his usual wary irony, cannot help but note that Diderot's vision of "the artist's independence" was subsumed, in the twentieth century, by his vision of art as "a moral and civic agent," leading to its use as "an instrument of despotism and a support of mediocrity" by such totalitarian and authoritarian societies as Nazi Germany and the Soviet Union. Perhaps Schapiro's most probing formulation of this paradox is his view that the doubleness or contradictoriness or precariousness of form in the best art is a sign of "searching conscience," as he calls it.[26] Creative originality is a form of searching conscience.

Schapiro's second paradox is that one can understand the past only through the present, a notion that he regards as a cliché of understanding. Nonetheless, it is suspect among traditional art historians because they do not see the spiritual continuity between the best traditional and the best contemporary art. Schapiro's attitude is that of Fromentin, one of his critic heroes: "Studying the works of the past, he strives to make himself contemporary with them as actions of a spiritual moment and a mood." This is why, like Fromentin, Schapiro "can speak . . . of the execution or colors or arrangement" of a work of art "as noble, generous, passionate, or candid," that is, "as possessing . . . the attributes of a superior humanity." In other words, art can embody a "full humanity."[27] Indeed, it can be more human than human beings, for they displace the hopes and aspirations they cannot realize onto it.

Schapiro's conception of the spiritual exchange that occurs between past and present art—an exchange that allows us to understand both more comprehensively and deeply than the traditional division of art history into disconnected and incompatible periods—is perhaps at its clearest in his argument that "modern practice disposes us to see . . . prehistoric works as a beautiful collective palimpsest." Schapiro believed that Berenson "failed to grow" "as a theorist and critic" because of his contempt for "contemporary taste in art" – he denounced "the whole of contemporary art as degenerate," not unlike the Nazis – even though "Berenson's aesthetic, with its categories of 'Form, Movement, and Space,' and his stern insistence on the highest values of art, seems in the line of thought which produced modern painting."[28] (They are the basics of visual art. The question for Schapiro is whether they are realized spontaneously and paradoxically, thus serving and symbolizing inner freedom, or whether they conform to some current orthodoxy's fixed conception of selfhood and society.) This is ultimately why Schapiro thinks Berenson is ridiculous as a thinker and even inauthentic as a connoisseur. Schapiro in fact cites several examples of major errors of attribution made by Berenson, casting doubt on his famous eye and his motivation for making the attribution. Many of the Renaissance works involved are not by the master's spontaneous hand, even to a novice eye. But in proclaiming that they were, Berenson increased their economic value – and his profit – enormously.

At its most literal, Schapiro's Jewish paradox asserts that Christian art can be understood only through Jewish spirituality and spontaneity. In fact, Christian art reifies the Jewish Bible into a dogmatic iconography. Even the idea of Christ is a reification of the Jewish idea of the messiah, a hopeful, spontaneous wish fulfillment. Christian art historians do not sufficiently realize the Jewish truth at the core of Christian art. It has to be emphasized that Christian art has been the dominant art of the West. It has absorbed every style and moral idea into its orthodoxy. Modern art, with its unorthodox emphasis on spontaneity and inner freedom rather than on blind faith in orthodox ideas, is a passing episode compared to orthodox Christian art. This is why Schapiro defends modern art, and unorthodox Christian art, so strongly.

Finally, consistent with himself, Schapiro is against Jewish orthodoxy – "the demands of [Jewish] ideological conformity" – as much as he is against Christian and capitalist orthodoxy.[29] This is why there is relatively little explicit mention of Jewishness in his writing. Jewish identity is as conflicted as Christian identity; that is, Jewishness is not a unified position, but a precarious balance of convictions. It is split in its vision of God: on the one hand, God is a wrathful if judicious patriarch; on the other hand, he is pure abstract creative spirit, able to manifest itself spontaneously in a flaming bush or a pillar of smoke. Schapiro preferred the latter conception: God's power was manifested neither in the punitive authority of patriarchy nor in matriarchy but in the pure grace of spontaneous creativity.

In this Schapiro is like Spinoza. One of the most interesting parts of Scha-

Alice Neel, Portrait of Meyer Schapiro, *1983. Oil on canvas, 42 × 32 1/8 in. (106.7 × 81.6 cm). The Jewish Museum, Purchase: S. H. and Helen R. Scheuer Family Foundation Fund, 1995-111. © Estate of Alice Neel, courtesy of Robert Miller Gallery, New York. Photograph by John Parnell © The Jewish Museum, New York.*

piro's essay on Berenson occurs when he expresses his disgust at the "grotesque comparison" Berenson makes between himself, Spinoza, and St. Paul. In contrast to Berenson they were, Schapiro writes, "two deeply dedicated and uncompromising Jews who, like himself, broke with the religion of their ancestors. But theirs was an act of courageous conviction, while for him the change of religion was a short-lived conversion that helped to accommodate him to a higher social milieu."[30] I believe that Schapiro, in his conception of art as a zone of spontaneity and inner freedom, was essentially a Spinozist. Like Spinoza he broke with Jewish orthodoxy out of courageous spiritual conviction in a creative God, even as, in his rabbinical habits of scholarship and his belief that art at its best is a kind of spiritual creativity—dare one say creation of spirit?—he showed that he was a dedicated and uncompromising Jew.

Like Spinoza he was a heterodox Jew who had a paradoxical conception of art—a conception that went back to Genesis, not to the orthodoxy of Mosaic law. Like Jewishness, art can be reduced to orthodoxy, ritual, rules, and materialism. But at its best it is divinely spontaneous and free, creative and inward in import. For Schapiro art is the realm in which the one true God becomes manifest. For him, as for many critic-aesthetes, art is a religion—a spiritual enterprise. It replaces traditional religion, which has lost its spirituality as it has become more and more orthodox and dogmatic.

I think that Schapiro was the last idealistic art historian-theorist-critic, certainly the last one who could even think of art as spiritual. But he expected more from art than it can give. Even at its best, art promises more than it can deliver; it is, after all, illusion, and illusion has never solved any world problems. Moreover, even the most spontaneous, creative, inwardly liberated art is full of orthodoxy and conformity, however much it keeps hope alive, but that alone is no mean feat. It would have been interesting to hear what Shapiro, so strong a defender of modern abstract art, would have thought of postmodern abstract art, which treats spontaneity ironically, satirizing and stylizing it, and regards inner freedom as a farce. Not only is modern art over, ironically because it has become orthodox and institutional, but the fact that it is routinely parodied and ironically manipulated suggests that it is despised.[31]

In general, the contemporary scene tends toward orthodoxy and conformity rather than spontaneity and spirituality. It is full of oppressive ideological demands that, whether they come from the left or the right, cannot help but suppress genuine creativity. The mind-controlling orthodoxies of the left and the right cannot help but produce aesthetically incompetent, not to say critically inadequate, art. For any orthodoxy—Christian, Jewish, Marxist, Freudian, feminist, multiculturalist, conservative, liberal, and so on—aesthetics is ultimately beside the point. For the orthodox, art is of use only to the extent that it reinforces ideological conformity. The orthodox prefer that it not be allowed to serve individualization and individuation—autonomy. But then aesthetically adequate art—art with the interiority and dialectical qualities Schapiro cherished—has always been rare.

Memoir

The iron cape of the Law, the gray
Thumb of the Word:
Careless of the mere spirit, careless
Of the body, ardent
Elders of the passion of the soiled, the charred.

Snuffboxes, smells of Europe.
Mr. Sokol crooning blessings
Absently to himself,
Neither the words nor the music,
Nothing of the mind and nothing
Of the senses but only
That one thing that shall come to pass
If you will hearken diligently with all
Your heart and all your soul and lay up these,

My words, inside your heart and in your soul
And bind them as a sign upon your hand
And they will be as frontlets between your eyes:
So we wrote the words on squares of lambskin.

And we sealed them in wooden boxes bound
In leather and threaded the boxes
On black leather thongs and bound the thongs
With the sealed words in appointed places
Around our heads and arms.
It was like saying: I am this, and not that.

And you shall teach these words
To your children, boxes
Bound at the heart and the eyes,
And you shall speak of them when you sit
Inside your houses and when you stand
Speaking in the marketplace, and bound
In your heart entirely when you walk the avenues
And when you go to bed
And when you arise.

Tin canisters of money, tumblers
Of memorial wax.
Necktie of Poland, shirt of grief. Chickpeas
And Seagram's whiskey, blessings of mousefur lapels.
That, and not this.

And you shall fasten
These words unto your doorposts and your gates
And so we did, in boxes
Put for a sign and a memorial
To you upon your hands and at your eyes
And in your hearts and in your houses and so we wrapped
The thongs and boxes with words inside them
Around our hands and arms and heads
And wore them as frontlets between the eyes
Through the shadows of summer
With so many turns of leather
Around the fingers of the hand
Nearest the heart.
And when your son
Comes to you saying *what is this*
You shall tell him of the slaying
Of the firstborn of man and of beast
In Egypt when my father came out of Egypt.

Alien as a blue carapace and a trident.
Unreadable
Totems, gilt fringes, varnished books. A horse chestnut
Throwing its massive summer shade
Over the pavement.

But ye that did cleave
Unto the Lord your God are alive,
Every one of you, this day.
Smells of wool and chickpeas,
The sandstone building converted now
To a Puerto Rican Baptist church,
Clerestory and minaret.
A few blocks away, an immense blue
Pagan, an ocean, muttering, swollen:
That, and not this.

—*Robert Pinsky*

SUSANNAH HESCHEL

The Myth of Europe in America's Judaism

SINCE the early nineteenth century American Jews, optimistic about the United States as a promised land whose political values are exemplified in Jewish thought, have creatively reimagined Judaism, both religious and secular. As the place of Jews in American culture changed, they re-created American Judaism with another place and culture in mind: Europe, which loomed as a mythic presence, sometimes a place of persecution, intolerance, and narrow-minded orthodoxy, at others a center of intellectual vibrancy and Jewish religious inspiration. The varying myths of Europe have shaped and inspired American Judaism to this day.

The Jewish experience in the United States is often regarded by rabbis and historians as one of growing assimilation and abandonment of Jewish identity. Lacking institutions of higher Jewish education, and without strong rabbinic leadership, the small American Jewish community in the first half of the nineteenth century did not participate in the explosion of scholarship and theological creativity that took place in Europe during the same period. Later in the century, the mass immigration of Eastern European Jews to the United States was perceived, in its day and subsequently, as an assimilation process: the immigrants and their children shed their religious observances, their distinctive dress, and their language. The rising rate of intermarriage between Jews and Gentiles in the late twentieth century seemed to give further proof that American Jews were abandoning their Jewish identity.

Yet assimilation, even conversion, its peak of expression, can create its own kind of psychosocial heritage. The initial group of Jews who arrived in Peter Stuyvesant's New Amsterdam in 1654 were Marranos, Jews who had converted to Catholicism under pressure from Spanish authorities and who often continued to practice Judaism in secret, or at least to maintain a surreptitious sense of Jewish identity. Their experience as Marranos, which was far from assimilationist, gave them a sense of social and political entitlement. In an essay celebrating the three hundredth anniversary of the arrival of the original twenty-three Jews in New Amsterdam, Salo W. Baron drew three important conclusions from this group's Marrano backgrounds that contradicted the assimilationist paradigm found in most of Europe.[1]

First, their practice of holding religious services in private during their early years in New Amsterdam—the first synagogue was not built on the American continent until the 1730s—is not surprising because that was what they had done as Marranos. Second, as Marranos in Europe they had adjusted to Christian conversion, holding significant roles as Christians in the government, the army, and the church, a practice that had accustomed them to positions of honor and authority, not subservience. Third, because they did not come from ghettos but were assimilated into Christian society, they were not about to take discrimination lying down. They fought against the anti-Jewish actions of the Dutch colonial director-general Peter Stuyvesant and they won. Even though subsequent generations of Jews in America did not come from Marrano backgrounds, the initial experience, Baron suggested, set a pattern of political and cultural self-assertion in America that was far more prominent than in Europe.

While the Marrano backgrounds of these early Jewish settlers spurred them to establish an American Jewish cultural and political life assertively different from what they had known in Europe, the past experiences of Jews in Europe nonetheless retained a forceful mythic presence in the minds of American Jews. Liberal rabbis and Jewish thinkers of the nineteenth and early twentieth centuries spoke of America not as posing an anti-Semitic or assimilationist danger but as offering the great hope for the Jewish future because American democratic principles embodied the true moral essence of Judaism. Only in America could Judaism come to its full fruition as a religion, they argued, because the absence of democracy in Europe encouraged discrimination against Jews and hindered their cultural self-realization. Indeed, America as a center of Jewish liberation became one of the guiding myths of the modern Jewish imagination. America in the eyes of modern Jews meant redemption from Europe, which symbolized both Judaism's subservience to Christianity and the confinement of Jews within the strictures of an unbending Orthodox Judaism. In the nineteenth and early twentieth centuries, American Jews thought of their Judaism as the authentic Judaism, a manly Judaism, while that of Europe was distorted by centuries of persecution and economic discrimination.

In the nineteenth century American Jews skillfully created an image of a Europe beset by intolerance and anti-Semitism, in contrast to America, the Jewish promised land. In dedicating a new Reform synagogue in Charleston, South Carolina, in 1841, Gustav Poznanski proclaimed, "This country is our Palestine, this city our Jerusalem, this house of God our temple." The Other was not only Europe, but European Judaism, which American Jews like Poznanski represented as oppressive, backward, and authoritarian. In fleeing Europe, the Jews who came to America could also flee Judaism. The Reform rabbi Samuel Adler, just after arriving in New York in 1857, declared, "Behind us lies Egypt, the Middle Ages, before us the sea of Talmudic legalism. . . . The spirit indwelling here in the West, the spirit of freedom, is the newly born Messiah." The goal, wrote Rabbi David Einhorn in his inaugural sermon in Baltimore in 1855, was "the liberation of Judaism for ourselves and for our children, so as to prevent their estrangement from Judaism."[2]

For Jewish thinkers, Protestantism could not stand alone in claiming a privileged place in America; Judaism, the original Israel, had to stand beside it as the religion informing the American democratic enterprise and bearing its own manifest destiny in the world. In an 1898 resolution, leaders of Reform Judaism in America declared that "America is our Zion. . . . The mission of Judaism is spiritual, not political . . . to spread the truths of religion and humanity throughout the world."[3] This was a Jewish echo of what Protestant thinkers, during and after the colonial period, had been doing: identifying the New Land with the Bible, and themselves with Israel. As Herman Melville declared in *White Jacket* (1850), "We Americans are the peculiar, chosen people – the Israel of our time; we bear the ark of the liberties of the world."

The sense of liberation that Jews experienced in America would also bring about a new kind of Jew. For the Reform rabbi Kaufmann Kohler, America would restore the Jewish "manliness" that life in Europe had undermined: America was "a country that rolled off the shame and the taunt[s] of the centuries from the shoulders of the wandering Jew, to place him, the former Pariah of the nations, alongside of the highest and the best, according to his worth and merit as a man."[4]

As much as Jews viewed America as an embodiment of Jewish values, they transformed Judaism in accordance with American principles into a religion of democracy. If European Judaism signified a backward-looking, Orthodox religiosity, Judaism in America meant freedom to develop a liberal religious expression by means of a democratic process. This entailed, for example, eliminating the role of chief rabbi, which dominated Jewish communities in Europe. It also meant strengthening the control of the laity over decisions regarding liturgy and ritual that in Europe had been under rabbinic authority. Mordecai Kaplan, the founder of Reconstructionist Judaism, expressed it: "The ancient authorities are entitled to a vote – but not to a veto," a radical repudiation of classical Judaism's authoritarian structure. Even Zionism, when it attained support from liberal Jews, was viewed as an essentially American phenomenon. For Louis Brandeis, Zionism not only was compatible with American Judaism but expressed the ideals of the Pilgrims, the American Revolution, and American democracy.[5]

The writings of nineteenth-century Reform rabbis energized Jewish thought in America. They failed to develop a formal theology, however, owing in part to the absence of institutions of Jewish higher learning and of an educated audience of laity, as existed in Europe. In addition, the rabbis' arrival coincided with an era of Christian revivalism that militated against theology. American evangelicals were, by the nature of their undertaking, uninterested in formal theology or intellectual debate and as a result, created no intellectual structure for their movement precisely at the time when German Protestants, by contrast, were reaching a pinnacle of sophisticated theological speculation. As Henry Steele Commager commented, "During the nineteenth century and well into the twentieth, religion prospered while theology went slowly bankrupt."[6]

The absence of an intellectual Christian theological tradition in the United States during the nineteenth century affected Jewish thought. There was no sophisticated academic community with which Jewish thinkers could engage and hone a formal Jewish theology. As a result, the publications of Jewish thinkers in the United States were not received by a critically attuned academic audience, in contrast to Germany, where Jewish thinkers found a lively (if critical, or even hostile) audience among their Christian counterparts.

This void also meant that no formally articulated Christian theological anti-Judaism was being developed (apart from whatever was transmitted from abroad, or from earlier theological writings), whereas in Germany, Christian theological denigrations of Judaism grew sharply in the nineteenth century and contributed significantly to negative perceptions of Jews. Such theological denigrations stemmed not only from rabble-rousing ministers like Adolf Stöcker, court preacher in Berlin, but also from scholars who claimed training in rabbinic literature, such as Emil Schürer. By contrast, the role of Christian theological seminaries in the United States was marginal to academic life, and while Stöcker was ranting against the emancipation of the Jews, American preachers were debating the abolition of slavery. Whatever negative attitudes toward the Pharisees or the Old Testament were held in common by German and American Christian ministers, they resonated considerably differently in the two political and cultural contexts. For example, in listing the various factors that shaped negative views of Jews in America, the historian Jonathan Sarna presents American Christianity as inhospitable to anti-Semitism, a conclusion inconceivable to a student of European Jewry.[7]

Various explanations have been offered for American Protestants' tolerance of Judaism: the Calvinists' appreciation of the Old Testament (in contrast to Lutherans' denigrations), the focus of Protestant hostility on Catholicism, the overriding preoccupation with slavery, and the problem of integrating numerous immigrant groups in addition to Jews. Unlike Europe, with its public and often violent anti-Semitism, America seemed a golden land of tolerance and opportunity for Jews. Yet that tolerance may not have been intentional or even deeply rooted in American culture but simply the result of an unusually low population density. Sidney Mead has observed that "there really was not much time in America for the traditionally antagonistic religious groups to learn to live together in peace. But there was space." Or, as Perry Miller writes, more cynically, Protestants "did not [willingly] contribute to religious liberty, they stumbled into it, they were compelled into it, they accepted it at last because they had to, or because they saw its strategic value."[8] If Jews had not been present in America, issues of religious tolerance would have revolved around Protestant acceptance of Catholics; the presence of Judaism stimulated a broader consideration of religious pluralism.

As Protestantism in America grew more nationalistic it did not turn to anti-Semitic racism as German Protestantism did. Religion, writes James Turner, "waxed fat and prosperous in the Gilded Age." The theological universalism of the era implied both a striving for Christian hegemony over the entire world, not just America, and also a belief in the "moral proprietorship over the nation." This was in striking contrast to the Christian theological justifications for imperialism developed in Germany, where the German *Volk* was elevated above all others, a Volk from which Jews were excluded. Indeed, the winds of *völkisch* theology began to blow stronger in Germany during the first decades of the twentieth century, until a *Volksnomostheologie* (people's theology) ultimately emerged as a dominant religious force within the Protestant church during the 1930s, according to which the German Volk was the measure of all things religious.[9] Religious teachings, such as the role of the Old Testament and the nature of Jesus, came to be measured according to these German Protestant theologians by their accord with the political and cultural interests of the racist nationalism that became National Socialism.

Christian claims inspired Jewish thinkers to assert competitively that not Christianity but Judaism held the rightful claim to a universal religious message. One of the most important figures in American Jewish thought, Kaufmann Kohler (1843–1926), became the spokesperson for liberal Judaism during that era after he arrived from Germany in 1869. In defining Judaism as essentially an "eternal moral idea" rooted in subjective experience, Kohler declared,

"The Bible is holy not because it is inspired, but because and insofar as it does still, inspire. It is not true because God has spoken the word, but because in the truth, the comfort, the hope, the final victory of justice which it holds out, you hear God speak to you in soul stirring strains." The goal of the Reform movement's Pittsburgh Platform, formulated by Kohler, was "to solve, on the basis of justice and righteousness, the problems presented by the contrasts and evils of the present organization of society," a formulation that encompassed the goals of the Protestant Social Gospel movement as well.[10]

Reform Jews identified the ills of modernity, but they did not reject modernization, technology, and rationalism. Instead they embraced modernity, as did Protestants, as a means to improve the world, to create God's kingdom on earth. Yet Kohler used a lofty bourgeois voice, like the voices of the liberal Protestants of his day, to direct contempt at Jewish displays of ethnicity, piety, and poverty. Kohler's Judaism was exclusive, disdainful of the massive influx of impoverished Eastern European Jewish immigrants who represented the medieval religious Judaism from which American Jews thought themselves liberated. The immigrants' arrival in the late nineteenth century introduced a wedge into the previous arrivals' comfortable identification of Judaism with America.

In "trumpeting a symbolic definition of self which Jews and Americans shared," as Arnold Eisen describes the effort, what was left of Jewish uniqueness, of the singularity of Judaism's religious message? Why be Jewish if simply being American represented the same thing? Since Judaism could not be identified by exclusive truths, Reform Jewish thinkers turned instead to the status of Jews. They defined Jewish chosenness not as indicating a supernatural quality inherent in Jews but as signaling an obligatory Jewish mission to spread biblical monotheism to the world. Even while touting the significance of the Jewish mission, however, Reform thinkers rejected Jewish nationalism, removing any hints of present-day or eschatological peoplehood from their liturgy and theology. The Reconstructionist Mordecai Kaplan, on the other hand, "intended to take the Jewish response to Emancipation represented by Kohler and carefully turn it on its head. . . . While the Reform Movement accepted chosenness in the form of mission and denied Jewish peoplehood, Kaplan did precisely the opposite. He accepted peoplehood and denied chosenness."[11]

The first major Jewish thinker in America who came from Eastern Europe rather than Germany, Kaplan represents a new stage in American Jewish thought: the introduction in American theological terms of the sense of cultural identity that was fundamental to European Jewish life. Like those in earlier generations, Kaplan sought to shape a Judaism distinctive to America by making Jewish values accord with American ones, but his emphasis was on Jewish culture, ethnicity, and nationhood, and he helped set the American foundations for Zionism. The story of the Exodus from Egypt, for example, functioned for Jews, Kaplan argued, the way the Declaration of Independence did for Americans.[12] America was not a melting pot but an opportunity to live in a Jewish subcommunity, a "cultural nationhood" that embodied the values of American democracy, to the extent that Americanism took precedence even over Judaism. Indeed, one of the motivations for his rejection of Jewish chosenness was democracy, which Kaplan, following John Dewey, viewed as a civil religion that helped people achieve self-realization, which for him meant salvation.

For Kaplan, understanding Jewish peoplehood as the central pivot of Jewish life made Judaism the creation of Jewish civilization, its "language and culture." He viewed Judaism's various religious manifestations as the *sancta*, the most important expressions of Jewish civilization through which the Jews expressed their identity, which functioned, in turn, to preserve their identity through centuries of diaspora. God, too, is such a sancta, and not the supernatural deity of traditional Judaism. Viewing Judaism as the product of Jewish civilization gave a historical impetus to Kaplan's cultural Zionism without suggesting a negation of diasporic life, and his dynamic view of Jewish society contributed to his endorsement of religious life as active, not passive. Kaplan and a growing number of Jews in the 1920s did not believe that Zionism would conflict with American Jewish loyalties, but would instead revitalize them.

The problem for American Zionists, like those in pre-1933 Germany, was the sense that they were already at home, not in the Diaspora. Yet the democracy that fostered their sense of being at home in America was precisely what endangered the Zionist dream, as did the possibility of a multiethnic democracy in Palestine that would include Arabs as well as Jews.

Following World War II, a broad disdain by intellectuals for all forms of nationalism arose in response to the course of National Socialism in Germany and undermined, in their eyes, the nationalist aspirationists of the Zionists. At the same time, Jewish optimism regarding America, and American Jews' desire to be liberated from the confines of European Judaism, ended, and in the second half of the twentieth century Jewish thought reversed itself. American Jews no longer believed that the United States was a place where Judaism could be nurtured or experience a renaissance. Instead, life in the United States became a source of worry, as it enticed Jews in ever larger numbers to assimilate and intermarry at rates that would soon lead to a sharp diminution in the size of the community. In addition, many secular Jewish intellectuals argued that post–

World War II America itself seemed to have lost its ideals and values and needed Judaism to save it from moral disintegration. In a reversal, American Jews no longer viewed Europe as a place of confinement but instead saw it as a source of inspiration that would help them rescue American Judaism from its moribund state. Moreover, many argued, America needed Judaism to rescue it from sinking into moral and political lethargy. Thus began the great reconception of the Marrano-American accord established in 1654. Instead of being Christian on the outside and Jewish on the inside like the Marranos, American Jews affirmed their identity in public as an expression of their internal commitments.

American Jews' involvement in the Civil Rights Movement was a watershed for their Jewish identity, both religiously and politically. No longer did Jews enter the political scene disguised as Christians – now they marched as Jews alongside African Americans. The photograph of Abraham Joshua Heschel marching in Selma has become iconic because it marks a watershed shift in American Jewish identity. Heschel noted at the time, "I am here because I am involved in the fate and dignity of my fellow man."[13] Judaism was no longer a religion practiced in secret, as it had been with the Marranos, but the very text of the movement in its identification with the Exodus and the Hebrew prophets. Jews were now fighting not for their own rights but for the rights of others and for the good of American society, a remarkable turning point in Jewish political history.

A significant number of rabbis who took part in the Civil Rights Movement were themselves refugees from Germany: Joachim Prinz, Ernst Lorge, Max Nussbaum, and Heschel, among others. These were people who had been repudiated by their own country, Germany, and wanted to express their dignity and their values in public political activism. Through the Civil Rights Movement, they enacted a rebuke of the Germans, showing how one ought to behave in a racist society and defining their Judaism through principles of justice, truth, and compassion. German and Eastern European Jews joined together in the movement, overcoming a long history of antagonism. Their alliance also made it clear that to be Jewish was to publicly express one's Jewish identity, rather than persist in the assimilationist traditions of Western Europe. The iconic impact of Heschel, with his beard and head-covering, marching at Selma with Martin Luther King, Jr., was derived from the visual impression Heschel made as a Jew.

For Heschel the inspiration for joining the Civil Rights Movement came from the prophets, while for others the turn to social justice was inspired by politics. Eugene Goodheart, in his memoir *Confessions of a Secular Jew* (2001),

Abraham Joshua Heschel (front row, second from right) in the Civil Rights march in Selma, Alabama, on March 21, 1965, with (front row, left to right) John Lewis, future U.S. representative from Georgia; an unidentified nun; Ralph Abernathy, cofounder of the Southern Christian Leadership Conference; Martin Luther King, Jr.; Ralph Bunche, undersecretary general for special political affairs at the United Nations; and Fred Shuttlesworth, founder of the Alabama Christian Movement for Human Rights. From the Ratner Center for the Study of Conservative Judaism, Jewish Theological Seminary, P898/N346.

describes the socialist movement he had been involved with before the war as a false progressivism that nonetheless imbued him with a sensitivity to social injustice that survived the movement's contamination by Stalinism.[14] For Heschel, however, there was no distinction between the religious and the political; he told me that in Selma he felt as though his legs were praying.

Religious inspiration, both for Heschel and for the younger generation of American Jews whom he inspired, was drawn not from the liberal movements of Central and Western Europe but from the pietistic movements of Eastern Europe, especially from Hasidism and its mystical traditions. The revival of neo-Hasidism in America in the 1960s led to major changes in the religious services of Reform, Reconstructionist, and Conservative synagogues, and to the creation of the Jewish Renewal movement, led by Arthur Waskow, Zalman Schachter, and Michael Lerner. Yet after World War II, Europe could no longer serve as a source of Jewish leaders, especially rabbis, even as it could no longer be held up as a paragon of culture and intellectual life for secular Jews. Younger, American-born Jews saw themselves as the saving remnant of European Jewry; but for the immigration of their parents and grandparents, they too might have perished. Others came here directly from the Displaced Persons camps of post-Nazi Europe. The Judaism they created tried to preserve the European legacy in an ethnic, particularist way, yet also with a universal message of political commitment to all people. Born after the war, mine is the generation that would not let the Jewish people disintegrate after the Holocaust. The revival of Judaism demanded reinterpretation; simply to preserve the old ways was "spiritual plagiarism," in Heschel's phrase.[15]

The assertiveness of the American Jewish legacy that Salo Baron noted in connection with the arrival of the first Jews in New Amsterdam led to dramatic innovations in Jewish religious life, particularly in the role of women in the synagogue and as ordained rabbis. Jewish feminism was a product of America, exported to Israel, Europe, and other diasporic communities, although it was not well received, even among liberal Jews. Yet the fight against discrimination, initiated by the first American Jews in protest of Peter Stuyvesant, inspired feminists in their struggle against Judaism's relegation of women to a secondary status.

While Jewish religious thinkers regarded European Jewish life as medieval and America as a place where Jews could be liberated not only from European anti-Semitism but from European Judaism, secular Jewish intellectuals turned to Europe as a suckling to its mother, seeking intellectual and political nourishment. For them America was crude and garish, the home of the "booboisie," in H. L. Mencken's phrase. In the 1920s Jews were not particularly well represented at American universities or other sites of intellectual exchange, and they looked instead to Europe as the seat of culture, politics, and intellectual refinement. European liberalism and Marxism were two of the strong currents that pulled the attention of Jewish intellectuals away from America. While modernity for Americans implied technological and economic progress, for Europeans it carried the taste of capitalism and commodification. Europe preserved the higher dimensions of human autonomy and fulfillment, the idea of freedom and culture, the utopia of a better life or at least a better education.

The admiration American Jewish intellectuals had for Europe came to an end with World War II. As a result, they had to drastically reconceive America. Europe, the source of intellectual life and the forefront of political advancement, was now the home of unbridled anti-Semitism, fascism, Stalinism, and the utter failure of liberalism, a failure that the philosopher Leo Strauss argued was no accident, but intrinsic to liberalism.[16] After all, it was liberalism that, despite having been the great supporter of Jewish Emancipation in Europe, had allowed the rise of the communism and fascism that had destroyed European Jewish life.

In a symposium held in the pages of *Partisan Review* in 1952, about a dozen American intellectuals, among them Leslie Fiedler, Philip Rahv, David Riesman, and Lionel Trilling, were asked to comment on their new regard for America and its institutions. "We have obviously come a long way from the earlier rejection of America as spiritually barren." "The end of the American artist's pilgrimage to Europe is the discovery of America," Fiedler wrote. Socialism ceased to figure in intellectual discussion, and American democracy, Rahv wrote, looked like the real thing: "At least [it] exists, not a mere theory or deduction from some textbook of world salvation."[17]

What is striking about the *Partisan Review* symposium is not just that the participants were all men but that Jews played a prominent role, even though they never articulated the word *Jew* or talked about Jewish interests. Religion played no role in the symposium. Personal affiliations were not disclosed. Nor did anyone discuss the implications of Nazism's defeat for Jews. The group praised the United States for its political freedoms, its economic strength, its traditions of nonconformity, its political security, and its avenues of social mobility. Yet they had concerns. David Riesman and Philip Rahv worried that the job of intellectuals—remaining in tension with their audience and milieu—would be difficult, given the comforts of American life and the embourgeoisement of the country's intellectuals. Trilling asked, "Where in American life can the artists and intellectuals find the basis of strength, renewal, and recognition, now that they can't depend on Europe as a cultural example?" There were the old Jamesian concerns about the barrenness of the native scene—"the flower of art blooms only where the soil is deep."[18]

They stood, in 1952, in the early years of a right-wing course away from socialism and communism and toward liberalism and neoconservatism. Irving Howe characterized the New York Jewish intellectuals in a 1969 essay as "the first group of Jewish writers to come out of the immigrant milieu who did not define themselves through a relationship, nostalgic or hostile, to memories of Jewishness."[19] Yet it is that very denial of a relationship to Jewish memory that came to be in itself a form of Jewish identity, much like the woman writer who says she is a writer, not a woman writer. Indeed, the New Criticism of the era sought to eliminate the biography of the author and focus on the ideal reader—

the Protestant white male as generic human.[20] Part of the reason was that in the postwar years the United States was uninterested in identity, universities were not particularly philo-Semitic, and modernism was elitist and anti-Semitic—think of the orthodox modernism created by the expatriates T. S. Eliot and Ezra Pound. The commitment to communism had had a religious intensity and its unmasking was a brutal experience, similar to what a later generation of Jewish feminists experienced in the unmasking of Judaism's patriarchy.[21] In both cases, the response contained a strong measure of conservative politics.

Even while secular American Jewish intellectuals turned away from Europe in the 1950s, many of them moving from socialism to neoconservatism, religious Jews turned increasingly toward the memory of Eastern European religious Judaism as a source of inspiration—yet they identified that Judaism with left-wing politics. What they were experiencing, however, was not their own memory of that vanished world, but a postmemory, to use Marianne Hirsch's term, a memory appropriated from their parents and grandparents.[22] That memory inspired a renaissance of Jewish creativity. Today it is no longer Europe that provides the inspiration for American Jews; Israel does that to some extent, but it is, primarily, America and American Judaism that offer political and religious inspiration to European Jews and, to some extent, to Israeli Jews. The major questions facing Jews have to do with multiculturalism, within both the community and the larger society; women's rights, which have brought the most radical changes in the synagogue since it was established; and the question of who is a Jew. On each of these questions, both European and Israeli Jews have remained negative, unable to respond to the challenges because their paradigms cannot cope.

Klaus Milich, a German scholar of American culture, has offered a useful distinction between the paradigm of modernity that has dominated postwar German and European thought—and Israeli thinking as well—and the paradigm of postmodernism that dominates American culture.[23] Whereas Europeans worry about the clash between cultures and civilizations, Americans attempt to expose the epistemological and ontological foundations of those antagonisms. In a similar fashion, we might observe that today's European Jewish communities think they can return to the structures of modernity: recognizing only Reform and Orthodox Judaism, retaining rabbis as the gatekeepers of their communities, and appealing to the state for protection against the anti-Semitism of the society. Within the American Jewish community, however, the concerns are with postmodernity: issues of cultural diversity are raised by feminism, critiques of Zionism, and multiculturalism.

In the United States the diffusion of Jewishness throughout popular culture and as a result of intermarriage has brought it to ever-increasing swaths of the non-Jewish population. Consequently, traditional Jewish boundaries and rabbinic determinations of Jewish identity have become unwieldy and meaningless. Postmodern America has invented a uniquely multiform Judaism, and the openness of America's multicultural society has encouraged a mixture of identities. American Jews are creating new forms of Judaism—Reconstructionist, Renewal, feminist—stemming from their interrogation and rejection of religious regimes of chosenness, patriarchy, authority, imitation of the Christian, and the old-fashioned modern; and they are participating in the restructuring of America as an immigrant, multicultural society that controls the state.

The older sense that Europe was in the forefront of modernization while the United States lagged behind has been altered. European intellectuals find themselves pallbearers of the Enlightenment while Americans theorize cultural diversity through poststructuralism, creating a useful model for Europe. Indeed, the flow of young Jewish intellectuals to Berlin since the mid-1990s has brought with it the introduction of postmodern paradigms that may help Germany come to grips with its increasingly multicultural society.

The American Jewish vision of Europe is no longer defined by confrontation with the Christian world but with the Muslim and Arab world on European soil, and with a resurgent anti-Semitism that reveals, yet again, the inability of European culture to cope effectively with it. Europe's only hope lies in following the American model of multiculturalism and radical democracy if it is to survive with its moral and political integrity intact. Similarly, the Zionism that originally developed as the repudiation of European anti-Semitism, as Arthur Hertzberg has argued, cannot now be blamed for European anti-Semitism.[24] Yet Zionism, too, like Europe, needs to be modified by the American political model and transformed from a repudiation of modern European culture into an embodiment of the principles of American democracy and multiculturalism.

The problematic side of postmodernism is its dissolution of boundaries and fixed identities, in which the cultural boundaries in America become so porous that Jewishness develops into a free-floating identity open to appropriation by anyone, including Jews. That is, Jewishness becomes staged, blurring the distinction between Jews and Gentiles, and obfuscating the nature of Jewish identity. Such staging is not unprecedented; at the Passover seder, for example, the liturgy demands that all Jews view themselves as if they had come out of Egyptian slavery and re-create the experience for a week.

While Jewishness is not an empty identifier—references to Israel, the Holocaust, holy days, and the Torah abound in American Jewish life, along with plenty of heroic political events – the act of being Jewish, whether Orthodox or secular, can become a performance. Just as the Marranos became outwardly Christian while remaining inwardly Jewish, American Jews also had to prove that they fit into the larger society, which, in the United States, was categorized by color. "White" and "black" were not only skin colors but social constructs and identifiers of social status. In yet another kind of performance, when Jewish vaudeville acts appropriated blackface in the early twentieth century they signified their entry into white American society. Michael Rogin has shown how blackface functioned to identify Jews with white America – only if one was white was it necessary to adopt blackface.[25] In a similar way, postmodernity leads American Jews to appropriate a "Jewface," a kind of *imitatio Iudei*, imitation of the Jewish.

The Marranos who came to these shores in the seventeenth century were strengthened by their experiences in Europe as Christians on the outside, Jews on the inside. They were able to establish themselves here successfully, while also teaching America how to become a pluralistic and tolerant society. Now it is Americans, having been inspired by their Jewish community, who can demonstrate to the rest of the world how a democratic, multicultural society can foster a flourishing Judaism.

Avenue

They stack bright pyramids of goods and gather
Mop-helves in sidewalk barrels. They keen, they boogie.
Paints, fruits, clean bolts of cottons and synthetics,
Clarity and plumage of October skies.

Way of the costermonger's wooden barrow
And also the secular marble cinquefoil and lancet
Of the great store. They persist. The jobber tells
The teller in the bank and she retells

Whatever it is to the shopper and the shopper
Mentions it to the retailer by the way.
They mutter and stumble, derelict. They write
These theys I write. Scant storefront pushbroom Jesus

Of Haitian hardware – they travel in shadows, they flog
Sephardic softgoods. They strain. Mid-hustle they faint
And shrivel. Or snoring on grates they rise to thrive.
Bonemen and pumpkins of All Saints. Kol Nidre,

Blunt shovel of atonement, a blade of song
From the terra cotta temple: Lord, forgive us
Our promises, we chant. Or we churn our wino
Syllables and stares on the Avenue. We, they –

Jack. Mrs. Whisenant from the bakery. Sam Lee.
This is the way, its pavement crackwork burnished
With plantain. In strollers they bawl and claw. They flourish.
Furniture, Florist, Pets. My mongrel tongue

Of *nudnik* and *criminentlies*, the tarnished flute
And brogue of quidnuncs in the bars, in Casey's
Black amber air of spent Hiram Walker, attuned.
Sweet ash of White Owl. Ten High. They touch. Eyes blurred

Stricken with passion as in a Persian lyric
They flower and stroke. They couple. From the Korean,
Staples and greens. From the Christian Lebanese,
Home electronics. Why is that Friday "Good"?

Why "Day of Atonement" for release from vows?
Because we tried us, to be at one, because
We say as one we traffic, we dice, we stare.
Some they remember that won't remember them –

Their headlights found me stoned, like a bundled sack
Lying in the Avenue, late. They didn't speak
My language. For them, a small adventure. They hefted
Me over the curb and bore me to an entry

Out of the way. Illuminated footwear
On both sides. How I stank. Dead drunk. They left me
Breathing in my bower between the Halloween
Brogans and pumps on crystal pedestals.

But I was dead to the world. The midnight city
In autumn. Day of attainment, tall saints
Who saved me. My taints, day of anointment. Oil
Of rose and almond in the haircutting parlor,

Motor oil swirling rainbows in gutter water.
Ritually unattainted, the congregation
File from the place of worship and resume
The rumbling drum and hautbois of conversation,

Speech of the granary, of the cloven lanes
Of traffic, of salvaged silver. Not shriven and yet
Not rent, they stride the Avenue, banter, barter.
Capering, on fire, they cleave to the riven hub.

—Robert Pinsky

Notes

BARBARA KIRSHENBLATT-GIMBLETT **Introduction**

1. Joseph Berger, "Salo Baron—Another Day's Work," *New York Times,* February 27, 1985, C20.
2. Salo Wittmayer Baron, *Ancient and Medieval Jewish History: Essays* (New Brunswick, N.J.: Rutgers University Press, 1972), 266.
3. *Facing the New World: Jewish Portraits in Colonial and Federal America,* The Jewish Museum, September 21, 1997–January 11, 1998.
4. Rachel Wischnitzer, *Synagogue Architecture in the United States: History and Interpretation* (Philadelphia: Jewish Publication Society of America, 1955), 13ff.
5. Max Weinreich, "The Reality of Jewishness Versus the Ghetto Myth: The Sociolinguistic Roots of Yiddish," in *To Honor Roman Jakobson: Essays on the Occasion of His Seventieth Birthday* (The Hague: Mouton, 1967), 2199–2211.
6. See Barbara Kirshenblatt-Gimblett, "The Kosher Gourmet in the Nineteenth-Century Kitchen: Three Jewish Cookbooks in Historical Perspective," *Journal of Gastronomy* 2, no. 4 (1986–87): 51–89, and Kirshenblatt-Gimblett, "Kitchen Judaism," in Susan L. Braunstein and Jenna Weissman Joselit, eds., *Getting Comfortable in New York: The American Jewish Home, 1880–1950* (New York: The Jewish Museum, 1990), 75–105.
7. "The Great Metropolitan Sanitary Fair," *Frank Leslie's Illustrated Newspaper,* April 23, 1864, 66.
8. This theme was taken up in the classic essay by Georg Simmel, "The Stranger," in *The Sociology of George Simmel,* trans. Kurt Wolff (New York: Free Press, 1950), 402–8.
9. I take this formulation from Olga Litvak, "Rome and Jerusalem: The Figure of Jesus in the Creation of Mark Antokol'skii," in Barbara Kirshenblatt-Gimblett and Jonathan Karp, eds., *The Art of Being Jewish in Modern Times* (Philadelphia: University of Pennsylvania Press, forthcoming).
10. Harold Rosenberg, "Is There a Jewish Art?" *Commentary* 42 (July 1966): 60.

ARTHUR HERTZBERG **Salo W. Baron and the Writing of Modern Jewish History**

1. I was moved to see that, when I gave this lecture at The Jewish Museum on April 14, 1996, the audience included such colleagues and disciples of Baron's as my contemporaries Henry Graff, who was chairman of the Columbia history department when Baron brought me in to teach modern Jewish history, and Isaac Barzilay, who was for many years professor of Hebrew and Hebrew literature at Columbia. It was a gather-

ing of a good number of us who grew up under Baron's influence and knew that we were the better for it.

2. Salo Wittmayer Baron, "The Modern Age," in Leo W. Schwartz, ed., *Great Ages and Ideas of the Jewish People* (New York: Random House, 1956).
3. Salo Wittmayer Baron, *A Social and Religious History of the Jews*, 3 vols. (New York: Columbia University Press, 1937); and Baron, *A Social and Religious History of the Jews*, 2nd ed., rev. and enlarged, 18 vols. (New York: Columbia University Press, 1952–93).
4. Baron, *Social and Religious History* (1952–93), 1:25.
5. Martin Buber, *Drei Reden über das Judentum* (Frankfurt am Main: Rütten und Loening, 1920).
6. This dissertation grew into my *French Enlightenment and the Jews* (New York: Columbia University Press, 1968).
7. Baron, *Social and Religious History* (1937), 2:432.

JONATHAN D. SARNA **"Facing the New World"**

1. Richard Brilliant, *Facing the New World: Jewish Portraits in Colonial and Federal America*, exh. cat. (New York: The Jewish Museum, 1997). For a review of the exhibition, see Ken Johnson, "Portraits That Conceal Identity," *New York Times*, October 24, 1997.
2. See David Hall, *Worlds of Wonder, Days of Judgment: Popular Religious Belief in Early New England* (Cambridge: Harvard University Press, 1989).
3. Leo Hershkowitz and Isidore S. Meyer, *The Lee Max Friedman Collection of American Jewish Colonial Correspondence: Letters of the Franks Family, 1733–1748* (Waltham, Mass.: American Jewish Historical Society, 1968), 60; and Edith B. Gelles, ed., *The Letters of Abigaill Levy Franks, 1733–1748* (New Haven: Yale University Press, 2004), 62.
4. Lionel D. Barnett, ed., *El libro de los acuerdos* (Oxford: Oxford University Press, 1931), 3.
5. Ibid., 15.
6. Yosef Kaplan, "Deviance and Excommunication in the Eighteenth Century: A Chapter in the Social History of the Sephardi Community of Amsterdam," *Dutch Jewish History* 3 (1993): 103.
7. Hershkowitz and Meyer, *Letters of the Franks Family*, 116, 119; Gelles, *Letters of Abigaill Levy Franks*, 123, 127.

BARBARA KIRSHENBLATT-GIMBLETT **The Moral Sublime**

I would like to thank Peter Cherches and Erin Mee for their able research assistance; Beverly Gordon for sharing her pioneering work on charity fairs with me; Grace Cohen Grossman, Senior Curator of Judaica and Americana at the Skirball Cultural Center and Museum, for her unfailing assistance; and Zachary Baker, formerly Senior Librarian, YIVO Institute for Jewish Research, now Judaica Curator, University Libraries, Stanford University; Abraham Peck, former director of the American Jewish Archives; and Steven Siegel, Archivist at the 92nd Street Y in New York, for directing my attention to useful material.

1. "The Story of Other Fairs," *American Hebrew*, December 27, 1895, 238. As Beverly Gordon has suggested, these events and their economic, social, and political importance have been underestimated by scholars (though their importance was certainly appreciated at the time). She attributes later dismissals of these events to the stereotype that they were run by housewives with time on their hands who made useless

fancywork for sale or supplied equally superficial bric-a-brac and other novelties. See Beverly Gordon, "Playing at Being Powerless: New England Ladies Fairs, 1830–1930," *Massachusetts Review* 27 (1986): 144–60. See also Mary Bosworth Treudley, "The 'Benevolent Fair': A Study of Charitable Organization Among American Women in the First Third of the Nineteenth Century," *Social Service Review* 14 (1940): 509–22; and Rodris Roth, "The New England, or 'Olde Tyme,' Kitchen Exhibit at Nineteenth-Century Fairs," in Alan Axelrod, ed., *The Colonial Revival in America* (New York: Norton, 1985), 159–83.

2. See Barbara Kirshenblatt-Gimblett, "Exhibiting Jews," in *Destination Culture: Tourism, Museums, and Heritage* (Berkeley: University of California Press, 1998).
3. David Philipson, ed., *Letters of Rebecca Gratz* (Philadelphia: Jewish Publication Society, 1929), 407–8; "The Educational Fair: Towards the Close," *Jewish Messenger*, December 20, 1895.
4. "The Educational Fair"; "The Fair as It Is to Be," *Jewish Messenger*, November 11, 1870.
5. For work that attends specifically to Jewish women's organizations and to German Jewish philanthropy during the nineteenth century, see "Jewish Women's Philanthropy," in Paula Hyman and Deborah Dash Moore, eds., *Jewish Women in America: An Historical Encyclopedia* (New York: Routledge, 1997); Maria Benjamin Baader, "Rabbinic Study, Self-Improvement, and Philanthropy: Gender and the Refashioning of Jewish Voluntary Associations in Germany, 1750–1870," and Tobias Brinkmann, "Ethnic Difference and Civic Unity: A Comparison of Jewish Communal Philanthropy in Nineteenth-Century German and U.S. Cities," in Thomas Adam, ed., *Philanthropy, Patronage, and Civil Society* (Bloomington: Indiana University Press, 2004); Faith Rogow, *Gone to Another Meeting: The National Council of Jewish Women, 1893–1993* (Tuscaloosa: University of Alabama Press, 1993); Riv-Ellen Prell, "The Vision of Woman in Classical Reform Judaism," *Journal of the American Academy of Religion* 50 (1982): 575–89; and Karla Goldman, *Beyond the Synagogue Gallery: Finding a Place for Women in American Judaism* (Cambridge: Harvard University Press, 2000). See also the Women in Philanthropy Web Site, University of Michigan, http://www.women-philanthropy.umich.edu/tributes/index.html.
6. An important exception is Beverly Gordon, *Bazaars and Fair Ladies: The History of the American Fundraising Fair* (Knoxville: University of Tennessee Press, 1998).
7. Hasia R. Diner, *A Time for Gathering, 1820–1880: The Second Migration*, vol. 2 of Henry L. Feingold, ed., *The Jewish People in America* (Baltimore: Johns Hopkins University Press, 1992), 102; Arthur Goren, *New York Jews and the Quest for Community: The Kehillah Experiment, 1908–1922* (New York: Columbia University Press, 1970).
8. Jacob Riis, "The Jews of New York," *Review of Reviews* 13 (1896): 58–62.
9. Strong, quoted in "The Fair in Progress," *American Hebrew*, December 13, 1895, 171.
10. *Our Daily Fair*, quoted in "The First Charity Fair," *Frank Leslie's Illustrated Newspaper*, April 30, 1864. On the history of sanitary fairs, see William Y. Thompson, "Sanitary Fairs of the Civil War," *Civil War History* 4 (1958): 51–57; Jeanie Attie, *Patriotic Toil: Northern Women and the American Civil War* (Ithaca: Cornell University Press, 1998); and Gordon, *Bazaars and Fair Ladies*.
11. Bertram W. Korn, *American Jewry and the Civil War* (Philadelphia: Jewish Publication Society of America, 1951), 98–107 (quotation, 103), provides a detailed account of the fund-raising activities of Jewish women during the Civil War and their participation in the sanitary fairs.
12. Ibid., 103, 105.

13. Ibid., 99.
14. *Jewish Messenger*, April 20, 1864.
15. "Town Topics," *Frank Leslie's Illustrated Newspaper*, April 16, 1864, 50.
16. Gordon, "Playing at Being Powerless," 154; "Town Gossip," *Frank Leslie's Illustrated Newspaper*, April 30, 1864, 82.
17. "Town Gossip," April 30, 1864, 66.
18. "The Hebrew Fair," *Jewish Messenger*, June 10, 1870; and "The Fair," *Jewish Messenger*, June 24, 1870. The author is comparing the Hebrew Fair with the Metropolitan Fair, a sanitary fair that was held in 1864, not 1863, as the author mistakenly asserts.
19. "The Fair," *Jewish Messenger*, October 21, 1870; "The Great Fair: Its Remarkable Success," *Jewish Messenger*, December 9, 1870.
20. The Purim balls were masked balls and, according to the *Jewish Messenger* (April 1, 1870), "the mask, in this country, seems to be affected solely by us Israelites" (1), particularly the practice of masked house visits on the holiday. On Purim balls, see Philip Goodman, "The Purim Association of the City of New York, 1862–1902," *Publications of the American Jewish Historical Society* 40, part 2 (December 1950): 135–72. On the role of immigrants, and in particular Germans, in teaching Protestant Americans how to have a good time, see David A. Gerber, "'The Germans Take Care of Our Celebrations': Middle-Class Americans Appropriate German Ethnic Culture in Buffalo in the 1850s," in Kathryn Grover, ed., *Hard at Play: Leisure in America, 1840–1940* (Rochester, N.Y.: Strong Museum, 1992), 39–60.
21. *Jewish Messenger*, February 8, 1895, 1; Leigh Schmidt, *Consumer Rites: The Buying and Selling of American Holidays* (Princeton: Princeton University Press, 1997).
22. Gordon, "Playing at Being Powerless," 153.
23. See "In a Wide Labor Field, What Is Now Accomplished by the Educational Alliance, Work of the Hebrew Institute," *New York Times*, May 19, 1895, 17. See also Adam Beller, *The Educational Alliance: A Centennial Celebration* (New York: Educational Alliance, 1990). This publication is unfortunately marred by errors. The Aguilar Free Library became part of the Seward Park Branch of the New York Public Library in 1906.
24. Isidor Straus, who led the family business, L. Straus and Sons, established Abraham and Straus with his brother Nathan in 1892, and acquired Macy's in 1896. He was an important philanthropist who, among his other achievements, created an endowment fund for the Jewish Theological Seminary. He and his wife, Ida, died in the sinking of the *Titanic*.
25. Isidor Straus, "President's Report," in Educational Alliance, *Annual Report*, 1895 (New York: Educational Alliance, 1896), 13; "Fair in Progress," 169.
26. Hewitt, quoted in "The Educational Fair: A Brilliant Opening," *Jewish Messenger*, December 13, 1895, 5; Educational Alliance and Hebrew Technical Institute, *Souvenir Book of the Fair in Aid of the Educational Alliance and Hebrew Technical Institute* (New York: De Leeuw and Oppenheimer, 1895), 44.
27. "An Educational Fair, Plans of the Hebrew Charitable Societies of the City to Have an Artistic Exhibition," *New York Times*, October 25, 1895, 16.
28. See Alan Trachtenberg, *The Incorporation of America: Culture and Society in the Gilded Age* (New York: Hill and Wang, 1982), and his more recent "The Incorporation of America Today," *American Literary History* 15 (2003): 759–64.
29. "The Hebrew Fair," *New York Times*, December 11, 1895, 6; Straus, "President's Report," 12. The *American Hebrew*, however, felt a need to defend the women against

charges of lack of idealism, adding to the observation of how lovely they were the commendation that they gave their all to the noble purpose of the fair. See "Fair in Progress," 171. In "Our Complaint Box," on page 174 of the same issue, a writer identified as a woman with the initials K.C.F. admonishes the women planning booths for the fair for not conducting their meetings in a businesslike way.

30. "Straus Diverts a Women's Meeting," *New York Times*, October 18, 1894, 7.
31. "Educational Fair: A Brilliant Opening," 5.
32. Ibid.
33. "Hebrew Fair," 6; and "Hebrew Fair Opens To-Night," *New York Times*, December 9, 1895, 2; "Our Gossip," *Jewish Messenger*, December 13, 1895, 1; "Educational Fair: A Brilliant Opening," 5.
34. "Educational Fair: A Brilliant Opening," 5.
35. Display advertisement, *New York Times*, December 19, 1895, 7; "The Great Hebrew Fair," *New York Times*, December 8, 1895, 20.
36. "Great Hebrew Fair," 20; "Educational Fair: Towards the Close." The gross sum and full table of receipts for the Educational Alliance fair were reported in the *American Hebrew*, December 27, 1895, 241. The net sum was recorded in the Educational Alliance's *Annual Report* for 1895, 13; "Our Gossip," 1. On the 1870 fair, see "The Hebrew Charity Fair," *Jewish Messenger*, December 23 and 30, 1870. "The Montefiore Home Fair," *New York Times*, December 12, 1886, 3.
37. "The Fair in Progress," *American Hebrew*, December 13, 1895, 171; "The Hebrew Fair," *New York Times*, December 15, 1895, 6.
38. "Educational Fair: Towards the Close."
39. Daniel J. Boorstin, *The Americans: The Democratic Experience* (New York: Random House, 1973); "Editorial Notes," *American Hebrew*, December 13, 1895; "Another Visit to the Fair," *American Hebrew*, December 20, 1865, 203; "Educational Fair: Towards the Close"; "Another Visit to the Fair," 204; "Editorial Notes"; "Our Gossip," 1.
40. See Barbara Kirshenblatt-Gimblett, "The Moral Sublime: The Temple Emanuel Fair and Its Cookbook, Denver 1888," in Anne L. Bower, ed., *Recipes for Reading: The Community Cookbook and Its Stories* (Amherst: University of Massachusetts Press, 1997); *Jewish Messenger*, December 6, 1895, 4.
41. "The Educational Fair," *Jewish Messenger*, November 22, 1865; "Fair in Progress," 171.
42. "The Educational Fair," *Jewish Messenger*, December 6, 1895.
43. "The Hebrew Fair," *New York Times*, December 17, 1865, 6; "The Hebrew Fair," *New York Times*, December 19, 1865, 7; "The Hebrew Fair," *New York Times*, December 21, 1865, 7.
44. "Fair in Progress," 169.
45. Arjun Appadurai, ed., *The Social Life of Things: Commodities in Cultural Perspective* (Cambridge: Cambridge University Press, 1986). On the history of American Jewish consumption, see Andrew R. Heinze, *Adapting to Abundance: Jewish Immigrants, Mass Consumption, and the Search for American Identity* (New York: Columbia University Press, 1990); and Jenna Weissman Joselit, *The Wonders of America: Reinventing Jewish Culture, 1880–1950* (New York: Hill and Wang, 1996).
46. See Anne Firor Scott, *Natural Allies: Women's Associations in American History* (Champaign-Urbana: University of Illinois Press, 1991). Scott traces the history of women's efforts from charity to reform, and from volunteerism to professional careers, from the 1790s to World War I.

ARIEL SEGAL **Jews of the Amazon**

1. Ariel Segal, *Jews of the Amazon: Self-Exile in Earthly Paradise* (Philadelphia: Jewish Publication Society, 1999).
2. Ibid., 3.
3. Ibid., 85.
4. Ibid.
5. Ibid.
6. Ibid., 196–97.
7. Ibid., 213.
8. Ibid., 1–2, 192–93.
9. Michael Freund, "Exodus from the Amazon," *Jerusalem Post*, September 11, 2003.

DONALD KUSPIT **Meyer Schapiro's Jewish Unconscious**

This essay was previously published, in slightly different form, in Donald Kuspit, *The Rebirth of Painting in the Late Twentieth Century* (New York: Cambridge University Press, 2000), 209–22, © 2000. Reprinted with the permission of Cambridge University Press.

1. Margaret Olin, "Violating the Second Commandment's Taboo: Why Art Historian Meyer Schapiro Took on Bernard Berenson," *Forward*, November 4, 1994, 23.
2. Harold Rosenberg, "Is There a Jewish Art?" in *Discovering the Present: Three Decades in Art, Culture and Politics* (Chicago: University of Chicago Press, 1973), 230.
3. Clement Greenberg, "Kafka's Jewishness," in *Art and Culture* (Boston: Beacon, 1961), 273.
4. Ibid., 270; Clement Greenberg, "The Impressionists and Proust," review of *Proust and Painting* by Maurice Chernowitz, *Nation*, August 31, 1946, 247.
5. Clement Greenberg, "David Smith's New Sculpture," *Art International* 8 (May 1964): 7.
6. Meyer Schapiro, "Chagall's Illustrations for the Bible" (1956), in *Modern Art: Nineteenth and Twentieth Centuries, Selected Papers* (New York: Braziller, 1978), 133, 121; Schapiro, "Cézanne" (1959), in *Modern Art*, 40; Schapiro, "Chagall's Illustrations for the Bible," 133.
7. Meyer Schapiro, "Mr. Berenson's Values" (1961), in *Theory and Philosophy of Art: Style, Artist, and Society, Selected Papers* (New York: Braziller, 1994), 225.
8. Olin, "Violating," 23.
9. Schapiro, "Mr. Berenson's Values," 225.
10. Ibid., 217, 222.
11. Max Horkheimer, quoted in Rolf Wiggershaus, *The Frankfurt School: Its History, Theories, and Political Significance* (Cambridge: MIT Press, 1994), 6, 4–5; Meyer Schapiro, "On the Aesthetic Attitude in Romanesque Art" (1947), in *Romanesque Art, Selected Papers* (New York: Braziller, 1977), 8; Schapiro, "The Sculptures of Souillac" (1939), in *Romanesque Art*, 104.
12. Schapiro, "The Nature of Abstract Art" (1937), in *Modern Art*, 186.
13. Schapiro, "Recent Abstract Painting" (1957), in *Modern Art*, 224; Schapiro, "On the Aesthetic Attitude," 1.
14. Schapiro, "Recent Abstract Painting," 215. Schapiro qualifies this more concretely:

"The pathos of the reduction or fragility of the self within a culture that becomes increasingly organized through industry, economy and the state intensifies the desire of the artist to create forms that will manifest his liberty in this striking [abstract] way" (222). It is worth noting that Schapiro follows Alois Riegl's method in finding "a necessary creative link" between Romanesque and modern abstract art (Schapiro, "Style" [1962], in *Theory and Philosophy of Art*, 78).

15. Schapiro, "Nature of Abstract Art," 193, 25.
16. For example, Schapiro, like Greenberg, emphasizes the "concreteness" of abstract art as well as its critical continuity with traditional art. See Schapiro, "Recent Abstract Painting," 217, 222.
17. Schapiro, "Sculptures of Souillac," 104.
18. Schapiro, "On the Aesthetic Attitude," 22; Schapiro, "Courbet and Popular Imagery: An Essay on Realism and Naïveté" (1941), in *Modern Art*, 73; Schapiro, "'Muscipula Diaboli,' The Symbolism of the Mérode Altarpiece," *Art Bulletin* 27 (1945): 185, 186; and Schapiro, "The Romanesque Sculpture of Moissac I" (1931), in *Romanesque Art*, 187–88.
19. Schapiro, "Sculptures of Souillac," 107, 113–14; Schapiro, "The Younger American Painters of Today," *Listener*, January 26, 1956, 147. In "An Illuminated English Psalter" (*Journal of the Warburg and Courtauld Institutes* 22 [1960]: 183), Schapiro observes that "the motif of the crossed legs is a general attribute of the ruler, whether good or evil; it isolates him from ordinary mankind, which sits or stands supported by both feet alike." It is perhaps the most exemplary instance of what Schapiro calls "chiasmic symmetry."

Schapiro pays a good deal of attention to the intense color contrasts that prevail in Cézanne's and van Gogh's paintings (*Paul Cézanne* [New York: Harry N. Abrams, 1965], 11–12; and *Vincent van Gogh* [New York: Harry N. Abrams, 1950], 19–22). This is not unlike the "intense . . . burning, heraldically bright . . . bands of contrasted color . . . spontaneous primitive" visionary color in the Beatus Apocalypse of Gerona, a medieval manuscript ("The Beatus Apocalypse of Gerona," *ARTnews* 61 [1963]: 50). In "From Mozarabic to Romanesque in Silos" (1939) (*Romanesque Art*, 35), he describes "Mozarabic painting as an art of color," using "constantly varied, maximum oppositions in the color through the contrasts of hue (and, to a lesser extent, of value)," and observes that in the Beatus manuscripts, "color is felt as a universal force, active in every point and transcending objects." It is worth noting that in his recurrent emphasis on "polar meanings," "polarity expressed through . . . contrasted positions," "polar structure," and "development between two poles" – to cite various references to polar thinking in his book *Words and Pictures: On the Literal and Symbolic in the Illustration of a Text* (The Hague: Mouton, 1973) and his essay "Style" – Schapiro strongly resembles Alfred North Whitehead. In *Process and Reality* (New York: Humanities, 1955), Whitehead argues that the "doctrine of multiple contrasts . . . when there are or may be more than two elements jointly contrasted" is "a commonplace of art" (349). He also writes, "The organism's" creative achievement of "depth of experience" involves "suppressing the mere multiplicities of things, and designing its own contrasts. The canons of art are merely the expression, in specialized forms, of the requisites of depth of experience" (483). Finally, Whitehead philosophizes that "the universe is to be conceived as attaining the active self-expression of its own variety of opposites – of its own freedom and its own necessity, of its own multiplicity and its own unity, of its own imperfection and its own perfection. All the 'opposites' are elements in the nature of things, and are incorrigibly there." They justify "the aesthetic value of discords in art" (531). It is in effect a "minor exemplification" (531) of major, universal opposites.

20. Meyer Schapiro and seminar, "The Miniatures of the Florence Diatessaron (Laurentian Ms Or. 81): Their Place in Late Medieval Art and Supposed Connection with Early Christian and Insular Art," *Art Bulletin* 55 (1973): 518.
21. Schapiro, "From Mozarabic," 83n87, 30; and Schapiro, "On the Aesthetic Attitude," 26n10, 9; Meyer Schapiro, "Mondrian: Order and Randomness in Abstract Painting" (1978), in *Modern Art*, 235; Schapiro, *Vincent van Gogh*, 29–30, 27, 22–23; Schapiro, *Paul Cézanne*, 12, 18, 27, 26; Schapiro, *Vincent van Gogh*, 8.
22. Schapiro, *Vincent van Gogh*, 34; Schapiro, *Words and Pictures*, 48. Meyer Schapiro, "On Geometrical Schematism in Romanesque Art" (1932), in *Romanesque Art*, 268.
23. Meyer Schapiro, "Freud and Leonardo: An Art Historical Study" (1956), in *Theory and Philosophy of Art*. See also, in the same book, "Further Notes on Freud and Leonardo" (1994). Schapiro's critique of Freud's psychoanalysis of Leonardo is eloquently epitomized in note 9 to "On the Relation of Patron and Artist: Comments on a Proposed Model for the Scientist" (1964) in the same book. Schapiro notes (237) that "Leonardo's slowness of work," which Freud interprets as "a neurotic sign," was a "more common characteristic [of artists] than Freud suspected. If one believes that Leonardo's failures to deliver were greater than those of other artists, it is also true that he has left us more writings, scientific observations, and technical inventions than any artist of the Renaissance, and perhaps of all time." Such slowness has to do with difficulties of creative work, not neurotic inhibition, although that may play a role.
24. Schapiro's "On Geometrical Schematism in Romanesque Art" takes as its point of departure Jurgis Baltrušaitis's *La Stylistique ornementale dans la sculpture romane* (Paris: Ernest Leroux, 1931), while his "Nature of Abstract Art" takes as its point of departure Alfred H. Barr, Jr.'s *Cubism and Abstract Art* (New York: The Museum of Modern Art, 1936).
25. Schapiro, "Recent Abstract Painting," 222.
26. Schapiro, "Mr. Berenson's Values," 222, 227; Meyer Schapiro, "Diderot on the Artist and Society," in *Theory and Philosophy of Art*, 206, 204, 205.
27. Schapiro, "Mr. Berenson's Values," 224; Meyer Schapiro, "Eugène Fromentin as Critic," in *Theory and Philosophy of Art*, 105.
28. Meyer Schapiro, "On Some Problems in the Semiotics of Visual Art: Field and Vehicle in Image-Signs," in *Theory and Philosophy of Art*, 6; Schapiro, "Mr. Berenson's Values," 212, 218, 219.
29. Schapiro, "On the Relation of Patron and Artist," 237.
30. Schapiro, "Mr. Berenson's Values," 211.
31. As early as 1967, Clement Greenberg, in "Where Is the Avant-Garde?" described modern art as "hypertrophied" and "institutional," later noting that "when everybody is a revolutionary the revolution is over" (*Modernism with a Vengeance, 1957–1969: The Collected Essays and Criticism* [Chicago: University of Chicago Press, 1993], 4:261–62, 299). Harold Rosenberg notes a similar "fashionabilizing" of the avant-garde, in "The Avant-Garde" (1969) (*Discovering the Present* [Chicago: University of Chicago Press, 1973], 86).

SUSANNAH HESCHEL **The Myth of Europe in America's Judaism**

1. Salo Wittmayer Baron, "Some of the Tercentenary's Historic Lessons," in Jeannette Meisel Baron, ed., *Steeled by Adversity: Essays and Addresses on American Jewish Life* (Philadelphia: Jewish Publication Society, 1971), 473–84.
2. Poznanski, Adler, and Einhorn, quoted in David Philipson, *The Reform Movement in Judaism* (New York: Macmillan, 1907), 467, 483, 481.
3. Jonathan D. Sarna, "Converts to Zionism in the American Reform Movement," in Shmuel Almog, Jehuda Reinharz, and Anita Shapira, eds., *Zionism and Religion* (Hanover, N.H.: Brandeis University Press, 1998), 189.
4. Kaufmann Kohler, "American Judaism," in *Hebrew Union College and Other Addresses* (Cincinnati: Ark, 1916), 198.
5. Mordecai M. Kaplan, *Not So Random Thoughts* (New York: Reconstructionist Press, 1966), 263; Sarna, "Converts," 198.
6. Commager, quoted in Sidney Mead, *The Lively Experiment: The Shaping of Christianity in America* (New York: Harper and Row, 1963), 55.
7. Jonathan D. Sarna, "American Anti-Semitism," in David Berger, ed., *History and Hate: The Dimensions of Anti-Semitism* (Philadelphia: Jewish Publication Society, 1986), 115–28.
8. Mead, *Lively Experiment*, 13; Miller, quoted ibid., 19.
9. James Turner, *Without God, Without Creed: The Origins of Unbelief in America* (Baltimore: Johns Hopkins University Press, 1985), 226; James H. Moorhead, *World Without End: Mainstream Protestant Visions of the Last Things* (Bloomington: Indiana University Press, 1999), xvii. The most prominent figure associated with *Volksnomostheologie* is Wilhelm Stapel, but for a broader study of its influence, see Wolfgang Tilgner, *Volksnomostheologie und Schöpfungsglaube: Ein Beitrag zur Geschichte des Kirchenkampfes* (Göttingen: Vandenhoeck u. Ruprecht, 1966). See also Cornelia Weber, *Altes Testament und völkische Frage: Der biblische Volksbegriff in der alttestamentlichen Wissenschaft der nationalsozialistischen Zeit, dargestellt am Beispiel von Johannes Hempel* (Tübingen: Mohr Siebeck, 2000).
10. Kohler, quoted in Michael Meyer, *Response to Modernity: A History of the Reform Movement in Judaism* (New York: Oxford University Press, 1988), 273n25. For the text of the Pittsburgh Platform, see *Encyclopaedia Judaica* (Jerusalem: Keter, 1971), 13: 571.
11. Arnold M. Eisen, *The Chosen People in America: A Study in Jewish Religious Ideology* (Bloomington: Indiana University Press, 1983), 6, 2.
12. Mel Scult, *Judaism Faces the Twentieth Century: A Biography of Mordecai M. Kaplan* (Detroit: Wayne State University Press, 1993), 252.
13. Abraham Joshua Heschel, personal communication to the author.
14. Eugene Goodheart, *Confessions of a Secular Jew: A Memoir* (New York: Overlook, 2001); Eugene Goodheart, personal communication to the author.
15. Abraham Joshua Heschel, *Man Is Not Alone* (New York: Farrar, Straus and Young, 1951), 164.
16. Leo Strauss, *Liberalism, Ancient and Modern* (New York: Basic, 1968); see also Shadia B. Drury, *Leo Strauss and the American Right* (New York: St. Martin's, 1997).
17. Newton Arvin et al., "Our Country and Our Culture: A Symposium," *Partisan Review* 19, no. 3 (1952): 283, 294, 304.
18. Ibid., 306, 314, 322–23; Henry James, quoted ibid., 305.

19. Ethan Goffman, "The New York Intellectuals and Beyond: Editor's Introduction," *Shofar*, March 22, 2003, 1; Howe, quoted ibid., 2.
20. Daniel R. Schwarz, "Eating Kosher Ivy: Jews as Literary Intellectuals," *Shofar*, March 22, 2003, 19.
21. Goffman, "New York Intellectuals and Beyond," 2.
22. Marianne Hirsch, *Family Frames: Photography, Narrative, and Postmemory* (Cambridge: Harvard University Press, 1997).
23. Klaus Milich, *Die frühe Postmoderne: Geschichte eines europäisch-amerikanischen Kulturkonflikts* (Frankfurt am Main: Campus, 1998).
24. Arthur Hertzberg, "Introduction," in *The Zionist Idea: A Historical Analysis and Reader* (Westport, Conn.: Greenwood, 1970).
25. Michael Rogin, *Blackface, White Noise: Jewish Immigrants in the Hollywood Melting Pot* (Berkeley: University of California Press, 1996).

Contributors

Rabbi Arthur Hertzberg (1921–2006) was Bronfman Visiting Professor of Humanities at New York University and Professor Emeritus of Religion at Dartmouth College. He is the author of numerous books, including *The Fate of Zionism: A Secular Future for Israel and Palestine* (2003), *A Jew in America: My Life and a People's Struggle for Identity* (2002), *The Jews in America: Four Centuries of an Uneasy Encounter: A History* (1989), *Being Jewish in America: The Modern Experience* (1979), and *Anti-Semitism and Jewish Uniqueness: Ancient and Contemporary* (1975). Over the past fifty years, Hertzberg served as a congregational rabbi, president of both the American Jewish Policy Foundation and the American Jewish Congress, and vice president of the World Jewish Congress.

Susannah Heschel is Eli Black Associate Professor of Jewish Studies in the Department of Religion at Dartmouth College, where she is also chair of the Jewish Studies Program. Among her many publications are *Abraham Geiger and the Jewish Jesus* (1998) and a forthcoming book, *The Aryan Jesus: Christianity, Nazis, and the Bible.* She has also edited several volumes, including *Moral Grandeur and Spiritual Audacity: Essays of Abraham Joshua Heschel* (1996) and *On Being a Jewish Feminist: A Reader* (1983). Professor Heschel has served as a Visiting Professor at Princeton University and the University of Cape Town.

Barbara Kirshenblatt-Gimblett is University Professor and Professor of Performance Studies at the Tisch School of the Arts at New York University, where she chaired the Department of Performance Studies for more than a decade. She is the author of *Destination Culture: Tourism, Museums, and Heritage* (1998) and a coauthor of *Getting Comfortable in New York: The American Jewish Home, 1880–1950* (1990), *Image Before My Eyes: A Photographic History of Jewish Life in Poland, 1864–1939* (with Lucjan Dobroszycki) (1977), and *Fabric of Jewish Life: Textiles from the Jewish Museum Collection* (1977). Professor Kirshenblatt-Gimblett is currently cochair (with Jeffrey Shandler) of the Working Group on Jews, Media, and Religion at New York University's Center for Religion and Media.

Donald Kuspit is an art critic and Professor of Art History and Philosophy at the State University of New York at Stony Brook. He is a contributing editor at *Artforum, Sculpture,* and *New Art Examiner;* the editor of *Art Criticism;* and the editor of a series on American art and art criticism for Cambridge University Press. The author of numerous articles, exhibition reviews, and catalogue essays, Professor Kuspit has written more than twenty books, including *The End of Art* (2004), *Redeeming Art: Critical Reveries* (2000), *Idiosyncratic Identities: Artists at the End of the Avant-Garde* (1996), *The Critic Is Artist: The Intentionality of Art* (1984), and *Clement Greenberg, Art Critic* (1979).

Robert Pinsky, former Poet Laureate of the United States (1997–2000), teaches in the Graduate Creative Writing Program at Boston University. His collection *The Figured Wheel: New and Collected Poems, 1966–1996* was nominated for the Pulitzer Prize in poetry and received the Lenore Marshall Poetry Prize and the Ambassador Book Award of the English-Speaking Union. Among his many other publications are the poetry collections *Jersey Rain* (2000), *The Want Bone* (1990), *History of My Heart* (1984), *An Explanation of America* (1979), and *Sadness and Happiness* (1975); a verse translation (1994) of Dante's *Inferno;* and the critical studies *Democracy, Culture, and the Voice of Poetry* (2002) and *Poetry and the World* (1988).

Jonathan D. Sarna is the Joseph H. and Belle R. Braun Professor of American Jewish History in the Department of Near Eastern and Judaic Studies at Brandeis University. He chairs the Academic Advisory and Editorial Board of the Jacob Rader Marcus Center of the American Jewish Archives and serves as chief historian of the National Museum of American Jewish History. Among the many books he has written or edited are *American Judaism: A History* (2004), *Women and American Judaism: Historical Perspectives* (2001), *The American Jewish Experience: A Reader* (rev. ed., 1997), *The Jews of Boston* (1995), *JPS: The Americanization of Jewish Culture* (1989), and *Jacksonian Jew: The Two Worlds of Mordecai Noah* (1981).

Ariel Segal, born in Venezuela and an Israeli citizen, is a scholar, journalist, and writer who received his Ph.D. in history from the University of Miami. He is the author of *Jews of the Amazon: Self-Exile in Earthly Paradise* (1999) and a book of short stories. He has been an international analyst for several radio networks, including the BBC and Kol Israel (the Voice of Israel), as well as a newspaper columnist. Segal lectures widely about Iquitos and about Zionism, Jewish history, mass media, international issues, and Latin America. He currently lives in Lima, Peru.

Index

Page numbers in *italics* refer to illustrations.

"ABC" (Pinsky), xii
Abernathy, Ralph, *99*
Abraham, image of, 13
Abstract expressionism, 73, 78, 79
Adler, Samuel, 93
Aguilar Free Library, New York, 44
Akiba ben Joseph, Rabbi, 16
Albo, Joseph, 24
Altruism, ethics of, 85
Amazon, tax-free region of, 67
Amazonian Jews, 5, 57–69
American Hebrew, 51, 52, 53–54
Amos, image of, 13, 15
"Antique" (Pinsky), 9
Arendt, Hannah, 15
Art: abstract, 73, 78, 79, 84; aesthetic character of, 85; breathing space for, 80–81; calculated ambiguity of, 81; classical style, 83; classification of, 83; commodification of, 79; creativity in, 76, 78–79, 80; double images in, 81–83, 85; full humanity embodied in, 85; as illusion, 88; Jewish paradox of, 76–81, 85, 86; originality in, 77, 80; orthodoxy in, 77, 78, 80, 87, 88; paradoxes of, 76, 77, 78, 79, 80, 84–85, 86; public recognition of, 80; as religion, 87–88; spontaneity and freedom in, 78–79, 80, 81, 83, 85, 86, 87; traditional vs. modern, 84, 85; visual, basics of, 86. *See also* Christian art; Modern art
Art history: aesthetic as separate from moral in, 84, 85; as Jewish science, 83; orthodoxy in, 83; Renaissance in, 84, 86; as study of dynamic dialectical process, 83
Assertiveness, legacy of, 8
Assimilation: of American Jews, 7–8, 65–66, 68, 91–92; conversion and, 92; dual identity and, 6, 7–8; immigration and, 7–8, 17, 19, 97; intermarriage and, 33, 91, 97, 103; Jewish disappearance by, 2, 7, 17, 18, 75; Marranos and, 3, 6, 65–66, 68, 92; as transformation, 19; in Western Europe, 98
"At the Fair" ("Robin"), 36
"Avenue" (Pinsky), 105–6

Bachman, Hannah (Einstein), 46
Baltrušaitis, Jurgis, 84
Barbados, Jewish community in, 29
Baron, Jeannette, 10, *14*, 23
Baron, Salo W., *10*, *14*, *22*; on anti-Semitism, 16, 19, 21; birth and early years of, 1, 11; *bitachon* as defining term for, 22–23; at Columbia University, 10, 12; death of, 10; as great rabbi, 24; on the Holocaust, 12, 15, 16–17, 19;

Baron, Salo W. (continued)
on the ideal life, 12; on Jews in New Amsterdam, 92, 100; mysticism of, 16, 20; on Nazi evil, 12, 15, 16, 19; on personal opinions vs. objective truth, 11, 16; as rationalist, 16
Baron, Tobey, 10
Baron family, 12
Barr, Alfred, 84
Barzilay, Isaac, 107n1
Belmont, August (né Schoenberg), 42
Belmonte, Marranos of, 66–67
Benamú Gonzales, Saul, 61
Bene Israel of Bombay, 66
Bento, Mr., 61
Berenson, Bernard: aesthetic of, 86; artistic qualities of, 81; Jewish characteristics of, 75, 76, 83; Jewish heritage repudiated by, 74–75, 79, 87; new identity created by, 75–76, 79, 87; qualities shared by Schapiro and, 75, 76, 83; as role model for Schapiro, 76; Schapiro's critical assessment of, 6, 74–76, 83, 84, 86, 87
Berger, Joseph, 1
Bernard, Saint, 82
Bialik, Hayim Nachman, 17
Bible: New Land identified with, 93; re-interpretation of, 17, 96
Birnbaum, Rabbi Eliyahu, 69
Bloomingdale, Joseph B., 49
Bombay, Bene Israel of, 66
Bon Marché, Paris, 38
Boorstin, Daniel, 51
Breathing space of work of art, 80–81
Brightside Day Nursery, New York, 53
Bronstein, Rabbi Guillermo, 67
Buber, Martin, 15
Bunche, Ralph, *99*
Bundists, 21

Campin, Robert, *Mérode Altarpiece*, 81
Cézanne, Paul, 73, 82
Chagall, Marc, 6, 73–74
Champfleury, 81
Charity fairs, 36–54; achievements of, 36, 40, 43–44; blockbuster, 37–38; children enlisted in sales force of, 50–51; in Civil War, 37–38, 41, 43; consumption as theme of, 51, 54; crowd as main attraction in, 48, *48*, *49*; department store as model for, 38, 41, 46, 49; English models of, 36; as falling out of fashion, 45, 50, 54; features of, 37, 44; fundraising via, 4–5, 36, 38, 39, 40, 43, 50; gift economy of, 49, 51, 54; Jewish, 37, 38–41, 43–54; religious themes of, 44, 51; souvenir books, *37*. *See also* Sanitary fairs
Chiasmatypy, 81, 83
Chiasmic dialectic, 81
Christian art: Jewish truth in, 86; Renaissance, 84, 86; Romanesque, 75, 76, 79, 82–83, 84
Christian revivalism, 94
Civil Rights Movement, 98–99, *99*
Civil War, U.S.: patriotism expressed in, 41; sanitary fairs and, 37–38, 41, 43
Columbia University, 10, 12
Commager, Henry Steele, 94
Communism, 102
Conference on Jewish Social Studies, 10
Confessions of a Secular Jew (Goodheart), 98–99
Creativity: in art, 76, 78–79, 80; as Jewish quality, 23, 76–78, 84; paradox of, 80, 85
Crows over the Wheat Field (van Gogh), 82
Curaçao, Jewish community in, 29

DeLancey, Oliver, 33
Department stores: Bon Marché, Paris, 38; charity fairs modeled on, 38, 41, 46, 49
Dewey, John, 97

Diderot, Denis, 81, 85
Diner, Hasia, 40
Discoordination, 81
Dohme Jews of Turkey, 66
Drei Reden über das Judcentum (Three addresses on Judaism) (Buber), 15
Duyckinck, Gerardus: *Jacob Franks* (attrib.), *31*; *Phila Franks* (attrib.), *32*

Edery Morales, Don Víctor, 62, 63–64, 65, 68
Educational Alliance: fair in aid of (*see* Fair in Aid of the Educational Alliance and Hebrew Technical Institute); formation of, 44–45; Jewish community and, 45, 46
Education Fair. *See* Fair in Aid of the Educational Alliance and Hebrew Technical Institute
Eichmann, Adolf, 15, 16
Einhorn, David, 93
Einstein, Albert, 17
Einstein, Mrs. William (Hannah Bachman), 46
Eisen, Arnold, 96
Eliot, T. S., 102
Emancipation, 2, 17, 18
Enlightenment, 17, 18, 103
Europe: absence of democracy in, 92, 93; anti-Semitism in, 94, 95, 101, 103; civilization in, 100; clandestine churches (*schuilkerken*) in, 30; cultural identity in, 96, 100–101; Displaced Persons camps in, 100; Jewish libraries of, 15; myth of, 91–104; pietistic movements of, 99; as source of inspiration, 98, 100, 102, 103

Facing the New World (Jewish Museum exhibit), 27, 33
Fair in Aid of the Educational Alliance and Hebrew Technical Institute (1895), 39, 40–41; business model of, 49–50; design of, 46, 47, 49; Jewish community and, 39, 40; post office of, *52*, 52–53; purposes of, 39, 45; religious themes in, 51; revenues from, 40, 50; sales force of, 50–51; size and scope of, 38–39, 44; *Souvenir Book*, *37*, 45–46, 47, *48*, *49*, 51, *52*; spectacles of compassion in, 53–54; voting contests in, 53
Fancy fairs, 54
Fiedler, Leslie, 101
Franks, Abigaill, 3, 28, 33
Franks, Jacob, *31*, 33
Franks, Phila, 3, *32*, 33
Freiman, Aaron, 11
Freud, Sigmund, 14–15, 84
Freund, Michael, 69
Fromentin, Eugène, 81, 85

Galicia, 12
Gauguin, Paul, 80
Germany: anti-Semitism in, 94, 95, 103; imperialism in, 95; Jews of, 21, 39, 44; multiculturalism in, 103; Nazis in (*see* Nazis); Protestants of, 94, 95; warring, 12
Gilded Age, 95
Ginzberg, Louis, 23
God, existence of, 20
Gomez, Lewis M., 30
Goodheart, Eugene, 98–99
Gordon, Beverly, 42
Goren, Arthur A., 40
Graff, Henry, 107–8n1
Grand Sanitary Fair (1864), 39
Gratz, Rebecca, 38
Great Ages and Ideas of the Jewish People (Schwartz), 12, 21
Great Hebrew Fair. *See* Fair in Aid of the Educational Alliance and Hebrew Technical Institute
Greenberg, Clement, 72, 73, 80–81

Ha'am, Ahad (Asher Ginsberg), 20
HaLevi, Yehuda, 69
Hasidism, 99
Hebrew Benevolent and Orphan Asylum Society, 39, 45, 50
Hebrew Fair. *See* Fair in Aid of the Educational Alliance and Hebrew Technical Institute
Hebrew Free School Association, 44, 45, 53
Hebrew Institute, New York, 45
Hebrew Orphan Asylum Society, New York, 39, 43, 53
Hebrew Technical Institute, New York, 44–45, 53–54. *See also* Fair in Aid of the Educational Alliance and Hebrew Technical Institute
Hegel, Georg Wilhelm Friedrich, 83
Herbert, Victor, 53
Hertzberg, Arthur, 1–2, 10, 103
Hertzberg, Phyllis, 10
Herzl, Theodor, 16
Heschel, Abraham Joshua, 18, 98–99, *99*, 100
Heschel, Susannah, 7–8
Heterodox: in art, 77, 78, 80; Jew as, 78; paradox of, 81
Hewitt, Abram S., 45, 48
Hirsch, Marianne, 102
Holocaust, 12, 15, 16–17, 19, 100
Holy Congregation Remnant of Israel, New York, 27, 28, 29–30
Horkheimer, Max, 78
Howe, Irving, 101

Ibn Verga, 69
"Immature Song" (Pinsky), 70–71
Immigrants. *See* Jewish immigrants
Impressionism, 79, 80
Inquisition, 61, 66, 67
Iquitos, Peru: Cohen and Company in, *58*; doorway with mezuzah in, 69, *69*; homogeneity of, 67; isolation of, 59; Jewish cemetery in, 57, 59, 60, *60*, 63, 67, 68; Jewish settlement in, 5, 57–69; Kabbalat Shabbat services in, 64–65; *kashrut* (dietary laws) observed in, 60–62; legends and myths in, 62, 63; Marranism of, 65–66, 68; multicultural influences in, 62–63, 65; secret code in, 60
Israel: establishment of, 20; inspiration of, 102; Jewish population in, 20; mission of, 14
Israeli Law of Return, 61, 67

Jacob Franks (attrib. to Duyckinck), *31*
Jamaica, Jewish community in, 29
James, Henry, 74
Jerusalem, destruction of the temple in, 17
Jeshuat Israel (Touro Synagogue), Newport, Rhode Island, 30, 46
Jesus: Amazonian Jews' beliefs about, 62–63, 68; and Jewish idea of messiah, 86
Jewish community, in nineteenth-century America: booths set up at sanitary fairs by, 41–42, 43; changing aspects of, 46; charity fairs of, 44, 45; Jewish identity in, 44, 104; public assembly of, 40–41; public image of, 39; solidarity expressed by, 39, 40–41; splits and fissures in, 40
Jewish Cultural Reconstruction, 15
Jewish Emancipation, 101
Jewish experience, triumph of, 12–13
Jewish identity: in Amazon region, 58–60; American (U.S.), 97, 98, 102, 103, 104; anxiety about, 72–73, 86, 97; artistic identity and, 73–74, 75–77, 78, 79; community expression of, 44, 104; conversion and, 66, 91; dietary laws and expression of, 60–62; isolation and, 58–60, 66; in multicultural societies, 59, 97, 102, 103, 104; paradox

of, 76–79, 85, 86; public expression of, 98; repudiation of, 74–75, 79, 87, 101; sanitary fairs as expression of, 41; social Judaism and, 44; survival and, 75, 76, 77
Jewish immigrants: assimilation of, 7–8, 17, 19, 66, 91, 97; Eastern European, 39, 40, 44, 91, 96, 98; German, 39, 98; Moroccan, 57; as targets of Christian missionary movement, 44
Jewish Messenger, 38, 43
Jewish mestizos, 5, 57, 59, 65–68
Jewish nationalism, 96
Jewish paradox, 76–81, 85, 86
Jewish pluralism, 8
Jewish Renewal movement, 100
Jewish Society of Iquitos, 5, 57, 59, 60, 62, 63
Jewish unconscious, 6
Jewish values, 97
Jews: alienation and, 73; anti-Semitism and, 16, 19, 21, 76, 92, 94–95, 101, 103; art and, 6–7, 75–77, 81; Ashkenazic, 67; assimilation of (*see* Assimilation); breathing space for, 81; centers of post-Holocaust populations, 20; community responsibility for, 28–30, 39, 40, 45; Conservative, 99; converting to Christianity, 42, 65, 74, 91, 92; creativity of, 23, 76–78, 84; deference as important value of, 28, 29, 30; dispersion of, 19, 28–29, 31, 97; double existence of, 6, 83; as the eternal people, 77; first exile of, 17, 19; German, 21, 39, 44; in ghettos, 18; halacha (body of Jewish law regulating all aspects of life), 19–20; Hasids, 99; *herem* (excommunication), 29–30; history of, 13, 15; identity of (*see* Jewish identity); intellectuals, 8, 97–98, 100, 101, 102, 103; intermarriage of, 33, 91, 97, 103; isolation of, 3; in Lima, 5, 59, 60, 67; morality of, 13–15, 18, 19, 20, 43, 54; in multicultural societies, 59, 97, 102–3, 104; Orthodox, 18, 86–87, 93; as Other, 78, 83, 93; philanthropy of, 4, 39, 40, 44, 45, 51, 54; portrait artists, 31–33; Reform, 18, 93, 94, 95–96, 99, 103; as representative people, 15; secular, 8; Sephardic, 28–29, 30, 33, 67; in Soviet Union, 20; survival of, 5–6, 8, 13, 17, 28, 57, 67, 75–77, 78, 81; traditional occupations of, 51; traditions of, 20, 28–29, 103; transformation of, 17, 19–20; in United States, 7–8, 20, 21–22, 91–104; visibility of, 3, 27; Zionists, 8, 20, 21, 93–94, 97, 102, 103
Jews of the Amazon (Segal), 57–59
Jews' Synagogue (Shearith Israel), New York, 27, 28, 29–30
Johnson, Samuel, 24
Joseph in Egypt, 13
Judaism: American (U.S.), 8, 91–104; European, 92, 96, 99–100; liberal, 95; moral essence of, 92, 95–96, 98; new, 17; obscure, 27; patriarchy of, 102; private practice of, 33; Reconstructionist, 8, 93, 96–97, 99, 103; revival of, 100; social, 44, 98–99; women's roles in, 100
Judenstadt (Herzl), 16

Kafka, Franz, 72–73
Kahal Kadosh She'arit Yisrael (Holy Congregation Remnant of Israel), New York, 27, 28, 29–30
Kaplan, Mordecai, 93, 96–97
Karo, Joseph, 24
Katzenellenbogen family, 18
King, Martin Luther, Jr., 98, *99*
Kohler, Kaufmann, 93, 95–96
Kohn, Annette, 52
Krochmal, Nachman, 15, 20
Kuspit, Donald, 6

Ladino, 28
Leonardo da Vinci, 84
Lerner, Michael, 100
Levy, Ronald Reategui, 68, 69
Lewis, John, *99*
Liberalism, 101
Lieberman, Saul, 23
London, Bevis Marks synagogue in, 30
Lopez, Aaron, 33
Lopez, Sarah Rivera (Mrs. Aaron), *27*
Lorge, Ernst, 98

Maimonides, 12, 21, 24
Manasseh ben Israel, 27–28
Marranism: conversion and, 92; Dutch, 7, 66; inspiration of, 7; as model of Jewish survival, 5–6; of natural assimilation in isolated communities, 3, 6, 65–66, 68, 92; in New World, 7–8, 65–66, 68, 91–92, 104; private religious services in, 92; self-assertiveness of, 92
Marrano-American accord (1654), 98
Marx, Alexander, 23
Marx, Karl, 17–18, 83, 100
"Material" (Pinsky), 25–26
Mead, Sidney, 95
Melville, Herman, 93
"Memoir" (Pinsky), 89–90
Mencken, H. L., 100
Mérode Altarpiece (Campin), 81
Messiah: coming of, 28; Jewish idea of, 86
Metropolitan Fair (1864), 41, 42
Metropolitan Museum of Art, New York, founding of, 38
Micah, 27
Milich, Klaus, 102
Miller, Perry, 95
Modern art: authentically creative, 76; identity as central issue of, 73–74; Jewish paradox in, 76; Nazi denigration of, 86; orthodoxy of, 86, 88; Schapiro on, 73–74, 79, 83–84, 86, 88; traditional vs., 84, 85
Modernism, 102
Mondrian, Piet, 82
Montefiore Home for Chronic Invalids, New York, 50
Moral sublime, 43
Morocco, Jews emigrating from, 57
Moses, 15
Moulin de la Galette (Toulouse-Lautrec), 80
Mount Sinai Hospital, New York, 39, 43, 50
"Mr. Berenson's Values" (Schapiro), 74–76
Multiculturalism, 59, 97, 102–3, 104

Nazis: art and libraries stolen and despoiled by, 15; art as instrument of despotism in, 85; Baron's thoughts on, 12, 15, 16, 19; defeat of, 101; on degenerate art, 86; racist nationalism of, 95, 97
Neel, Alice, *Portrait of Meyer Schapiro, 87*
Neoconservatism, 101, 102
Neoimpressionism, 79, 80
New Amsterdam, Jews in, 7–8, 40, 91–92, 100
New Criticism, 101
Newport, Rhode Island, Jeshuat Israel (Touro Synagogue) in, 30, 46
New York Jews: *kehillah* established (1908), 40; sanitary fairs of, 39–40; self-sufficiency of, 40
Nietzsche, Friedrich, 15, 81
Nussbaum, Max, 98

Olin, Margaret, 72, 74
"On a Line of Hart Crane's" (Pinsky), 55–56
"On the Humanity of Abstract Painting" (Schapiro), 84
Openness, law of, 14

Oppenheim, Moritz Daniel, 51
Orthodox iconography, 80
Orthodoxy: aesthetics as beside the point in, 88; in art, 77, 78, 80, 87, 88; in art history, 83; authoritarian tendencies of, 84; breathing space from, 81; of Christian art, 86; conflict behind, 83; extreme, as fascism, 84; intense feeling as critical of, 79; Jewish, 86–87; paradox of, 81; in religion, 88; spontaneity as rebellion against, 78, 80; survival and, 78, 79
Other, Jew as, 78, 83, 93
Ottoman Empire, Sephardim of, 28
Our Daily Fair, 41

Palestine, multiethnicity in, 97
Paradox: in action, 81; in art, 76, 77, 78, 79, 80, 84–85, 86; of art history, 84; in doubleness of form, 85; of meaning, 82; of originality, 77, 78; spiritual liberation via, 77–79; of understanding the past through the present, 85–86
Partisan Review, 101
Paul, Saint, 87
Peruvian Amazon, 57
Phila Franks (attrib. to Duyckinck), *32*
Pinsker, Leo, 16
Pinsky, Robert: "ABC," xii; "Antique," 9; "Avenue," 105–6; "Immature Song," 70–71; "The Material," 25–26; "Memoir," 89–90; "On a Line of Hart Crane's," 55–56; "Samurai Song," viii; "Shirt," 34–35
Pittsburgh Platform, 96
Poland, Jewish people in, 21
Portrait of Meyer Schapiro (Neel), *87*
Portuguese Congregation, New York, 37
Portuguese Jewish "nation," 28–29
Postmodern abstract art, 88
Postmodernism, 102, 103, 104
Poststructuralism, 103
Pound, Ezra, 102
Poznanski, Gustav, 92–93
Prinz, Joachim, 98
Progressive Era, 44
Protestants: religious tolerance of, 7, 95; Social Gospel movement of, 96; theological speculation of, 94
Psychoanalysis, 83–84
Purim Association, 44

Rahv, Philip, 101
Reategui Levi, Ronald, 68, 69
"Recent Abstract Painting" (Schapiro), 84
Recife, Brazil, Jewish community in, 29, 32
Reconstructionists, 8, 93, 96–97, 99, 103
Remnant of Israel synagogue, New York, 27, 28, 29–30
Renaissance Christian art, 84, 86
Riegl, Alois, 83
Riesman, David, 101
Riis, Jacob, 40
Rogin, Michael, 104
Romanesque art, 75, 76, 79, 82–83, 84
Rosenberg, Harold, 7, 72, 73
Rothschild family, 42

"Samurai Song" (Pinsky), viii
Sanitary fairs: art exhibitions in, 42, 46; as art form, 43; Civil War and, 37–38, 41, 43; department store as model for, 41, 46, 49, 51; as expression of democracy, 45; as expression of Jewish identity, 41; as fundraising events, 4–5, 36, 38, 39, 40, 43, 50; Jewish community and, 39–42, 51; Jewish symbolism in, 47, 51; men in charge of, 46–47; as model for other fairs, 41, 43; moral sublime captured in, 43; organizations represented in booths of, 41–42, 43; women participating in, 4, 42–43, 46–47. *See also* Charity fairs

Sarah Rivera Lopez (Mrs. Aaron Lopez) (Stuart), 27
Sarna, Jonathan D., 2, 94
"Scenes from Jewish Life" (Oppenheim), 51
Schachter, Zalman, 100
Schapiro, Meyer, 6–7, 72–88, 72, *87*; on art as religion, 88; on autonomy, 80; on Berenson, 74–76, 83, 84, 86, 87; on breathing space, 80–81; on calculated ambiguity of art, 81; on commodification of art, 79; on discoordination, 81; on doubleness of art, 81–83, 85; on images of force, 82; on innovation as a Jewish quality, 75; on Jewish identity, 73–77, 83, 86; on Jewish nature of art, 76–77, 81, 86; on juggling, 82; on modern abstract art, 73–74, 79, 83–84, 86, 88; on paradoxes of art history, 84–86, 87; on paradoxes of meaning, 82; on paradox of originality, 77–79, 80; on Romanesque art, 75, 76, 79, 82–83, 84; *Selected Papers*, 72, 75; on spontaneity and inner freedom, 81, 83
Schmelzer, Menahem, 11–12
Scholem, Gershom, 20, 23
Schürer, Emil, 94
Schwartz, Leo, 12
Segal, Ariel, 5–6
Self-Portrait (Schapiro), 72
Servatius, Robert, 16
Seurat, Georges: *Study for Le Chahut*, 80; *A Sunday on La Grand Jatte – 1884*, 80
Shearith Israel "Jews' Synagogue," New York, 27, 28, 29–30
"Shirt" (Pinsky), 34–35
Shoah, 12, 15, 16–17, 19, 100
Shuttlesworth, Fred, *99*
Social and Religious History of the Jews (Baron), 1, 2, 12, 15, 19, 20, 23
Socialism, 101, 102
Sodom, destruction of, 13
Soviet Union: art as instrument of despotism in, 85; Jews in, 20
Spinoza, Baruch, 86–87
Stalinism, 99, 101
Stöcker, Adolf, 94
Straus, Isidor, 45, 46, 49
Straus, Nathan, 46–47
Strong, William L., 41
Stuart, Gilbert, *Sarah Rivera Lopez (Mrs. Aaron Lopez)*, 27
Study for Le Chahut (Seurat), 80
Stuyvesant, Peter, 92, 100
Sunday on La Grand Jatte – 1884 (Seurat), 80
Surinam, Jewish community in, 29
Symbolists, 80

Talmud, 17
Third Commonwealth, 21
Thomas Aquinas, Saint, 24
Thorndike, Lynn, 23
Torah, study of, 12
Toulouse-Lautrec, Henri de, *Moulin de la Galette*, 80
Touro Synagogue (Jeshuat Israel), Newport, Rhode Island, 30, 46
Trilling, Lionel, 101
Turkey, Dohme Jews of, 66

Ukraine, German conquest of, 12
United Hebrew Charities, 45
United States: absence of theology in, 94; anti-Semitism in, 21, 94; Civil Rights Movement in, 98–99, *99*; democratic principles of, 92, 93, 101, 103, 104; early Jewish life in, 7–8, 27, 30–33; Gilded Age in, 95; Jews in, 20, 21–22, 91–104; modernity in, 100, 103; myth of liberation in, 92; postwar rethinking of, 100–102; as promised land, 91, 92–93; Reform Judaism in, 93; religious tolerance in, 7, 95; revivalism in, 94; social mobility in, 101;

society based on color in, 104; vaudeville in, 104; Zionism in, 94
United States Sanitary Commission, 38, 41, 43

van Gogh, Vincent, 73, 80, 82; *Crows over the Wheat Field*, 82
Vásquez, Jaime, 62, 63, 64–65
Volksnonostheologie (people's theology), 95

Washington, George, 45–46
Waskow, Arthur, 100
Weinreich, Max, 3
Weizmann, Chaim, 17
Whitehead, Alfred North, 113n19
Wischnitzer, Rachel, 3
Wise, Stephen S., 1
Wittmayer patrimony, 12
Wolfson, Harry A., 23
Women: careers for, 54; and circulation of wealth, 54; fancy fairs run by, 54; feminism, 102, 103; and Jewish fairs, 44, 50–51; as ordained rabbis, 100; and philanthropy, 36; public appearances of, 42, 43; rights of, 102; roles of, 100; sanitary fairs organized by, 4, 42–43, 46–47
World's fairs, 38
World War II, 12, 19, 76, 97–98, 100–101

Young Men's Hebrew Association (YMHA), 44, 45, 51

Zionists, 8, 20, 21, 93–94, 97, 102, 103

The Jewish Museum Board of Trustees